*A Garland Series*

# RENAISSANCE DRAMA

## A COLLECTION OF
## CRITICAL EDITIONS

edited by
STEPHEN ORGEL
The Johns Hopkins University

A Critical Edition of
THE TRUE TRAGEDY OF
HEROD AND ANTIPATER
by Gervase Markham and William Sampson (1622)

GORDON NICHOLAS ROSS

GARLAND PUBLISHING, INC.
NEW YORK & LONDON • 1979

COPYRIGHT © 1979 BY GORDON NICHOLAS ROSS

ALL RIGHTS RESERVED


All volumes in this series are printed on
acid-free, 250-year-life paper.


Library of Congress Cataloging in Publication Data

Markham, Gervase, 1568?– 1637.
  A critical edition of The true tragedy of Herod and
Antipater.

  (Renaissance drama)
  Originally presented as the editor's thesis, University of
Florida, 1969.
  Bibliography: p.
  Includes index.
  1. Herod I, the Great, king of Judea, d. 4 B.C. —Drama.
I. Sampson, William, 1600?– 1655? joint author.
II. Ross, Gordon Nicholas, 1940–      III. Title.
IV. Title: The true tragedy of Herod and Antipater.
V. Series.
PR2659.M3H4  1979      822'.3      78-66833
ISBN 0-8240-9734-3


PRINTED IN THE UNITED STATES OF AMERICA

In 1962 F. N. L. Poynter wrote of _Herod_ and _Antipater_: "It is not as well known as it deserves to be, for, unlike many worse plays of the period, it has never been reprinted" ("Gervase Markham," English Association _Essays_ and _Studies_, XV, 27-39). Despite its obscurity, the play continues to receive occasional critical attention, and I hope the present edition will enable it to become more widely known.

In recent years two critics have made mention of _Herod_ and _Antipater_. Leonora Leet Brodwin, in _Elizabethan_ _Love_ _Tragedy_ _1587-1625_ (1971), classifies the play properly as a chronicle history and not a love tragedy. (She is mistaken, however, in thinking that A. C. Dunstan edited the play.) Of greater interest is an article by Leah Scragg, "Shakespearian Influence in _Herod_ and _Antipater_" (_Notes_ and _Queries_, July 1968). In this the author shows that Antipater is in many ways reminiscent of Shakespeare's Edmund. Cited in evidence are the bastardy of the two villains, similarities in their aims and methods of deception, other resemblances between the plots of _Herod_ and _Antipater_ and _King_ _Lear_, and a number of verbal parallels in the two characters' speech. Scragg speculates: "It may well have been the similarity between the situations of the Antipater of the source and the Edmund of the newly re-published _Lear_ [the second quarto, 1619] which led the dramatists to expand Antipater's role into that of the aspiring bastard, departing from the source...." This may have been so. Yet since the play apparently existed in some form as early as 1613--a fact that Scragg seems unaware of--the influence may have derived from the original quarto of _Lear_ (1608).

Readers of <u>Herod</u> <u>and</u> <u>Antipater</u> may be interested in two other recent articles which treat matters related to it. In "To Out-Herod Herod: The Development of a Dramatic Character" (<u>Comparative</u> <u>Drama</u>, Spring 1976), David Staines provides an excellent study of the Herod of the medieval drama. Finally, Philip J. Ayres offers evidence that Sampson's only other surviving play was produced ("almost certainly in a truncated and debased form") as late as 1733--"Production and Adaptation of ... <u>The</u> <u>Vow</u> <u>Breaker</u> (1636) in the Restoration" (<u>Theatre</u> <u>Notebook</u>, Summer 1973).

CONTENTS

# INTRODUCTION

## I.  Markham and Sampson and their Works

The True Tragedy of Herod and Antipater (STC 17401-2) was
published in 1622 by Mathew Rhodes (see below, p. xxxi ) as the joint
effort of Gervase Markham and William Sampson, Gentlemen.  Concerning
these authors little is now known.  Of the biographical sketches of
Markham, the best is certainly that by F. N. L. Poynter, from whose
account the following facts are drawn.[1]

Markham was born in Nottinghamshire around 1568.  He received a
good education, probably at Cambridge, and studied Latin, French,
Italian, Spanish, and perhaps even Dutch.[2]  His knowledge did not stop
here, however, for Markham was always an avid student of country matters.  "Yet did I for nine yeares," he once wrote, "apply my selfe to
the plow."  From this experience Gervase gained a close familiarity
with agrarian and rural lore.  He was from his youth, moreover, an excellent horseman, and once he even entertained the queen with a display of skillful riding (Poynter, pp. 9-10, 14).

During the last decade of the 16th century Markham became a
soldier and also began his career as a poet.  There is also evidence
that in these years the young man tried hard to become accepted into
the Essex party.  His early poetical works, which began to appear in

---

[1] For the Notes to the Introduction please see p. 176.

1593, are all dedicated to members of Essex's circle. One of the poems, Devoreux, or Vertues teares (STC 19793, dated 1597), is ostensibly in honor of the Earl's brother, killed in battle at Rouen in 1591. Yet the real object of Markham's praise is not the dead, but the living Essex, whom the poem flatters embarrassingly.[3]

As a poet, however, Markham produced no great work. Eight of his poems survive, three of them treating religious subjects and a fourth recounting the celebrated last fight of the Revenge. Perhaps because he felt that his poems were not being well received, Markham began to diversify his literary interests. In 1608, in collaboration with Lewis Machin, he turned out the first of his two dramatic attempts. This was a comedy called The Dumbe Knight (STC 17398), about which Hazlitt has justly said that "its merits are by no means conspicuous."[4] Markham kept trying, nevertheless. Finding time for belles lettres in prose, he produced six works of varying genres. In this category his best effort is perhaps The English Arcadia (in two parts--1607 and 1613: STC 17351-2), a continuation of Sidney's romance.

For none of his literary works, however, is Markham remembered. His reputation instead rests on his practical manuals. He is credited with over a dozen books on a wide range of subjects--husbandry, domestic economy, rural occupations and pastimes, military training and discipline, and most importantly, horsemanship and veterinary medicine. These last, the horsebooks, must have had an enviable reception, for they went through many editions and continued to be authoritative manuals into the 19th century.

In spite of the popularity of these manuals, though, Markham fell into poverty in his last years. He died at about 69 years of age

iv

on February 3, 1637, and posthumously received the dubious epithet of being the "first English hackney writer."[5]

The facts concerning William Sampson are scant, the following summary being taken from Sir Sidney Lee's Dictionary of National Biography notice. Sampson, like Markham, was a Nottinghamshire man by birth. Again like Markham, William probably spent his youth in service at one of the local great households, but of his formal education no record exists. As a man Sampson acquired a permanent position as a retainer of Sir Henry Willoughby, a baronet of Derbyshire. Beyond this fact virtually nothing is known about his life except that it ended, a year before Markham's, in 1636.[6]

Sampson's literary output seems to have been negligible. Aside from his share in Herod and Antipater, all we know to have come from his pen are three poetical works and two other plays. Only one volume of Sampson's poetry was ever published, this appearing in 1636 as Virtus post Funera vivit, or Honour Tryumphing over Death, being true Epitomes of Honourable, Noble, Learned, and Hospitable Personages (STC 21687). The work contained 32 verses in heroic couplets praising various figures, as well as a strong plea for the patronage of William Cavendish, the Earl of Newcastle (DNB, XVII, 723). Of the two other dramatic works only one survives. This is The Vow Breaker (1636: STC 21688), a representation in tragic form of an incident that supposedly occurred locally in Nottinghamshire. The play concerns a broken betrothal, the suicide of the jilted fiancé, and his ghost's driving the vow breaker to join him in death. Though essentially melodramatic, the situation nonetheless has the makings of worthwhile drama; yet Sampson's handling of it is at best mediocre. The other play, unluckily among those destroyed by Warburton's servant, might well have been better. As a comedy entitled The Widow's Prize, it was licensed in 1625 by Herbert, who noted that it contained "much abusive matter" and allowed it only "on condition, that my reformations were observed."[7]

## II.  A Synopsis of "Herod and Antipater"

In order for much of the remainder of this introduction to be clear, the reader may wish to know at this point the basic plot of the play:

Herod, King of Judah, learns that his mother-in-law and her son, the High Priest, are attempting to flee his court in fear of his tyranny. With feigned affection he pardons them. Then, as he himself plans a journey, he privately binds Antipater, his bastard son, to carry out two commands: to murder the High Priest; and to kill Marriam, his queen, should Herod die while away. Joseph, Herod's brother-in-law, overhears this promise. Antipater, alone, reveals his own ambition for the throne and plots the death of all who block his way.

When the High Priest is drowned, Joseph tells Marriam of Herod's two commands. Meanwhile, Antipater leads Salumith, Herod's sister and wife of Joseph, to think that her husband and Marriam are lovers. When Herod returns, Salumith accuses the queen of adultery. At the same time Pheroas, Herod's cup-bearer, falsely accuses Marriam of urging him to poison the king. Herod sends Marriam and Joseph to death, but then, too late, he grieves for her loss.

Now Salumith and Antipater contrive four separate plots against Herod's two rightful sons, whom he kills despite their innocence. He next sends Antipater to Rome so that Augustus can confirm him in the succession. Before leaving, the bastard entrusts Pheroas and Salumith with poison to be used on Herod; but when Pheroas dies, the king discovers the plot and Antipater's true nature. When the false son returns, Herod condemns him to the block. In the face of death Antipater betrays Salumith as his accomplice. Then, as the fatal blow falls, Herod also dies, overcome with grief.

### III.  Sources, Analogues, and Influences

The question of the source of _Herod and Antipater_ involves a curious red herring. On the title page of 1622, the authors identify their source as "the learned and famous Jewe Josephus." Again in the prologue, credit is given to "Josephus th'ancient writer." In fact the events related in Josephus's life of Herod (_The Jewish Wars_, Bks. I-II, and _The Jewish Antiquities_, Bks. XIV-XVII) closely resemble those in the drama. Yet that Josephus was the main source for the playwrights is almost certainly incorrect.

This fact was first pointed out by A. M. Silbermann in a study entitled _Untersuchungen über die Quellen des Dramas The True Tragedy of Herod and Antipater_ (Wittenberg, 1922). Here Silbermann shows that instead of Josephus, the playwrights depended primarily upon an abridgement that first appeared in 1558 under the following impressive title:  _A Compendious and most marveilous history of the latter tymes of the Jewes commune weale, beginnynge where the Bible or Scriptures leave, and continuing to the utter subversion and laste_ destruction of that countrey and people: Written in Hebrew by Joseph Ben Gorion, a noble man of the same countrey, who sawe the most thinges him selfe, and was auctour and doer of a great part of the same. Translated into Englishe by Peter Morwyng... (STC 14795).

Would the matter were this simple. Instead, as Silbermann shows, Morwyng was himself either mistaken or deliberately misleading. Evidently he took the name Joseph ben Gorion to be another form of the name Josephus (Silbermann, pp. 18, 32ff.). Yet this was not the case, since Josephus lived in the 1st century and Ben Gorion did not abridge his work until the 10th. Even so, as if to make confusion worse confounded, Morwyng did not in fact translate Ben Gorion's work, but--again as Silbermann proves--actually translated a 16th-century Latin history derived from Ben Gorion. The editor of this Latin version, dated 1559, was named Sebastian Lepusculus.[8]

Thus the main source of Herod and Antipater was really a far cry from Josephus. There were, in fact, six intermediate steps between Josephus and Markham and Sampson, as the following chart drawn up by Silbermann (p. 20) demonstrates:

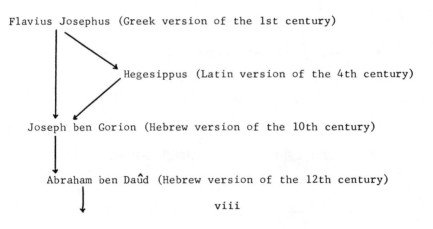

Flavius Josephus (Greek version of the 1st century)

Hegesippus (Latin version of the 4th century)

Joseph ben Gorion (Hebrew version of the 10th century)

Abraham ben Daûd (Hebrew version of the 12th century)

$\downarrow$

Sebastian Münster (Hebrew version with a Latin translation
of 1529)

Sebastian Lepusculus (Hebrew version with a Latin translation of 1559)

Peter Morwyng (English translation of the Latin version)

It will not be practical here to summarize the evidence offered
by Silbermann in support of this derivation, since the proof requires many pages of careful comparisons (see Silbermann, pp. 15-33).
Of further value, I hope, will be the "Appendix Concerning Sources"
which follows the text of the play in the present edition on p. 211.

There is still another area of study important to the reader
of Herod and Antipater. In a work entitled The Tragedies of Herod
and Mariamne (New York, 1940) Maurice J. Valency catalogues and compares more than 35 plays analogous to that of Markham and Sampson.
These plays are all derived ultimately from Josephus's history and
treat essentially the same material as Herod and Antipater. They
range in dates of composition from 1552 to 1938, and include among
their authors such names as Philip Massinger, Roger Boyle (the Earl
of Orrery), Voltaire, Elijah Fenton, and Friedrich Hebbel. Six of
these tragedies are worth mentioning here because they were written
before Herod and Antipater and were thus conceivably known by its
authors. Listed chronologically, these are:

1. Hans Sachs, Tragedia der Wütrich König Herodes (1552)

2. Lodovico Dolce, Marianna (c. 1560)

3. William Goldingham, Herodes Tragoedia (c. 1567)

4. Lupercio Leonardo de Argensola, La Alejandra (c. 1585)

5. Alexandre Hardy, Mariamne (c. 1600)

6. E. C. [Elizabeth Carew?], The Tragedie of Mariam (1613).[9]

Of these six the best in many respects is that by Hardy. Also
remarkable is Hans Sachs's play, since it is structured much the
same as Markham and Sampson's. In practically all of the other
dramas described by Valency the death of Mariamne is deferred until
the fifth and final act. In Sachs's play, however, as in the text
we are editing, Mariamne dies in the second act, leaving the rest
of the play to deal with the struggle between Herod and Antipater.
E. C.'s tragedy may also be noteworthy because of its classical
regularity and observance of the unities. None of these six plays,
nevertheless, had any noticeable influence on Markham and Sampson,
and in fact no evidence exists to show that the authors of Herod and
Antipater knew them. They may have, but they borrowed nothing from
them.

Indeed, only in a few general matters--aside from Morwyng--
does there seem to be evidence of influence on Herod and Antipater.
First is the striking similarity between Act I, scene v (the "slave
scene") of our play and a scene in Massinger and Dekker's play
The Virgin-Martyr (1622: STC 17644). Because the latter play was
written in 1621 before Herod and Antipater was published, one would
assume that Markham and Sampson borrowed from Massinger and Dekker.
Yet, oddly, the indebtedness probably worked the other way.
Silbermann (p. 47), comparing the phrasing of the two scenes, de-
cides that Markham and Sampson's was written first. Other evidence

x

in favor of this decision involves the date when <u>Herod</u> and <u>Antipater</u> was most likely composed, a factor that Silbermann does not consider. Concerning this date more will be said under section IV below. For the similar passage from <u>The Virgin-Martyr</u> see p. 199 of the Notes of Explanation and Comparison.

A more likely influence is Sallust's <u>War of Jugurtha</u>, from which the dumb show involving Jugurth and his brothers (II.i.605ff.) seems to be derived. Since Sallust's history had been translated in 1608 by Heywood,[10] it is possible that Markham and Sampson relied on this version for their material. Assuming this to be the case, I have included the passage from Heywood's Sallust in the notes on p. 202.

Strongly felt also is the influence of Seneca. Among the elements that seem conspicuously Senecan are the various ghosts and Furies, the sensational deeds of violence and blood, the numerous <u>sententiae</u> in the dialogue,[11] the stoical warnings against passion,[12] and the summarizing of off-stage events via the messenger's report.[13] Antipater's strange soliloquies are likewise Senecan, both in style and content. A frequent device in Seneca's plays is the long mono-logue wherein someone plots a course in villainy or revenge. In this type of speech the speaker often invokes supernatural aid, usually that of the Furies. Antipater's speeches are clearly of this type: not only does he call on the Furies ("Come...and bee mid-wives"),[14] but now and then he echoes the idiom of some of Seneca's plotters, as the present Notes of Comparison point out. In general, too, Antipater's lines are flavored with the mythological lore that permeates Seneca's plays; and we see finally that one of

the dumb shows (I.iii.373ff.) presents the climactic events of Seneca's
Agamemnon. We can be sure, moreover, that the playwrights knew this
particular play since the two Latin lines of advice given to Antipater
(I.iii.403 and 406) come from it.

Finally, another pervasive influence on Markham and Sampson is,
not surprisingly, Shakespeare. Throughout Herod and Antipater lines
from the master playwright are echoed, many of which are cited in the
present notes. Further influence of Shakespeare may be evident in
the character of Antipater (see p. xxvii below),[15] in the ghostly
business of V.ii.107ff. (see p. xxxi below), and possibly in the
use of Josephus as a chorus, similar to Gower in Pericles.

## IV.  Date and Manner of Composition

Although Herod and Antipater was first printed in 1622, it
may have existed in some form as much as ten years earlier.  In
1613, in an epistle to another work, Markham referred to his
Herodias, a title which seems applicable only to the play we now
have.  If the play was indeed written by that date, as Poynter
argues (p. 62), then in its earliest form Herod and Antipater was
almost surely the product of Markham's single authorship.[16]  J. Q.
Adams, Jr. stresses this point:  "'In 1612,' says the D.N.B., 'William
Sampson, either the dramatist himself, or his father, figured among
the humbler owners of land' in South Leverton, a village near Retford,
Nottinghamshire.  Later he became a retainer in the family of Sir
Henry Willoughby, and with the leisure which this position gave him,
was enabled to turn his attention to literature."[17]  This evidence
is not conclusive, of course, but it is persuasive.  The likeliest

solution seems therefore to be that Sampson was asked to revise
Markham's play for performance, probably around 1621. This is
Poynter's suggestion (p. 61), which is, I believe, essentially cor-
rect.

Another factor pointing to this conclusion is the likelihood
that Markham's earlier play, The Dumbe Knight, was composed in this
fashion: Markham wrote the first draft alone, and this was probably
later turned over to Lewis Machin for revision. The distinct contributions of the two authors seem clear in this case, as Adams has
shown (MP, X, 413-32). In the case of Herod and Antipater, however,
the portions belonging to Markham and to Sampson are nearly impos-
sible to distinguish.

V.  The Place of the Play in the Dramatic
Tradition; and the Artistry of the Play

Herod and Antipater is one of many Jacobean plays that ana-
lyzed the problems of statecraft. Like the chronicle plays of the
Elizabethan stage, the Jacobean group was directed toward an audi-
ence very much interested in government. In one central respect,
however, the latter plays differed from the former: whereas the
older chronicle plays had dealt with English history, the Jacobean
plays treated mainly foreign politics; and while many of the chronicle plays had dramatized recent history, the plays under King James
often reached back to more ancient times.[18]

One may puzzle over this change in subject matter. Of the
factors that may have operated, three or four seem especially
likely. First is the possibility that the English chronicle play

reached the natural limit of its development by practically exhaust-
ing the annals on which it was based. The Tudor playwrights had
shown the times and troubles of every English king since the
Conquest.[19] Shakespeare alone had covered everything, seemingly,
from the fall of Richard II to the rise of Henry VII. Thus, with
much of the native history already presented, the Jacobean authors
may well have turned to foreign matter to find fresh inspiration and
interest.

A second obvious factor is the great change in the national
spirit that came with the beginning of the 17th century. One can
hardly ignore the fact that the chronicle plays faded in popularity
just as the days of Elizabeth were drawing to a close.[20] With her
passing and the coming of James, the great zeal of patriotism that
had marked England since 1588--and that had fostered nationalistic
drama--waned. The doubt and fear concerning the Succession, and then
the new Scots sovereign's inability to inspire confidence in his subjects, cast a somber pall over the country.

In another way, too, James's policies may have contributed to
the change in the political plays. The new king had not been in
England two months before he began to issue patents that were to
bring theaters, players, and playwrights entirely under State control.[21] No longer were any noblemen permitted to keep companies of
players; rather, companies were now to be sponsored only by members
of the royal family. Designed in part to protect the theaters from
attacks by the Puritans and by the city magistrates, these measures
may nevertheless have been adverse to the drama in the long run. By
the second decade of the 17th century, at any rate, the new vogue

sought to gratify the aristocratic and artificial tastes of the Court. Seemingly as a result, fewer new plays presented subject matter of any national interest.[22]

Censorship measures were also tightened. Allusions to current political events were not encouraged. Not that James was a fearsome tyrant, but he was headstrong and unpredictable. When in 1624 Middleton's play A Game at Chess ridiculed one of the issues closest to James--the collapse of the proposed alliance with Spain that James had so long favored--the king let his displeasure be known.[23]

For a number of reasons, then, the Jacobean playwrights may have thought it expedient to turn to non-British subject matter, especially if they wanted to comment obliquely on current English politics.[24] In some cases elaborate parallels seem to have been worked out in the plays, so that the action apparently offered a sustained commentary on topical events--by way of veiled analogy.[25] Such may have been the intention of Herod and Antipater.

As explained above (p. xii ), the play may have been written as early as 1612 or as late as 1621. In either case the basic parallel of the analogy would seem apparent: the play presents an autocratic, foreign-born king who invites trouble through his unwise and unstable policies.[26] Assuming this much as intended, what further resemblances might we find between the events in the play and those in England during the years in question? If the play did originate by 1612, Markham could possibly have foreseen what would happen following the death of Salisbury in that year--notably, that such favorites would arise as Somerset and Buckingham.[27] If he were such a prophet, Markham may therefore have meant to project in Antipater some of the dangers to the realm that such powerful personal advisers might pose.

Certainly such analogy is possible if Markham or Sampson undertook revision of the play during the period from 1613 to 1621. These were often shameful days under James. The scandal that ruined Somerset was his wife's hand in the murder of Sir Thomas Overbury. Many in the realm had already looked askance at Frances Howard's divorce from the Earl of Essex so that she could marry Somerset. Overbury's mistake was in opposing the marriage. Imprisoned on a token charge by James, Sir Thomas was evidently poisoned in 1613, but some two years passed before the crime was traced to Lady Somerset.[28] When she confessed to having ordered it, Somerset was himself widely thought to have shared the guilt. But perhaps the most shocking moment was yet to come, when--both having been sentenced to death-- James stepped in to pardon them.[29]

Next, however, Buckingham was raised to prominence by James, and this young star quickly became malign. In no time Buckingham grew so full of his new power that he would not tolerate anyone in court who had not been advanced by him. As one historian grimly observes, "Buckingham exacted servility from all, and honest criticism and outspoken advice were no longer heard in James's court."[30] Surely the flavor of this statement, as well as of the events reviewed here, might easily suggest the court of Herod as Markham and Sampson depicted it. Or, turning the relationship around, the dark events of the play would seem to reflect such real disgraces as the execution of Raleigh in 1618--merely to placate Spain--and the flurry of impeachments that arose in these years--such as that which toppled

Bacon in 1621.[31]  In broadest terms, therefore, the Jacobean audiences

should have been able to see in the play whatever they wanted to.

Aside from these possibilities, Herod and Antipater is no great

tragedy, and the reasons for this are possibly three.  First is the

"chronicle-wise"[32] technique of linear narrative, with the action mov-

ing from incident to incident in a manner often confusing and disuni-

fied.  Second is the blurred focus of the play, giving the effect of

two stories instead of one--that of Herod and Marriam, which ends with

her death in the second act, and that of Herod and Antipater, which

continues through the remainder of the play.  But the third defect of

the play is far more damaging than either of the foregoing and thus

should be considered in detail:  the play lacks a clearly defined theo-

logical framework.

We can begin exploring this aspect by observing the world in

which the action unfolds.  The world, if Herod's court can be taken as

an emblem of it, is characteristically that of the greatest Jacobean

tragedies--a degenerated world, decayed with evil and far removed from

the Golden Age of the past.[33]  Like that of King Lear, it is a world

where the natural order is turned topsy-turvy, where "Natures best

chaine" (II.i.433)--that binds husbands to wives and fathers to sons--

is broken, and where a bastard given to ambition would not hesitate to

"obscure the world, and spoyle / Both man and beast, Nature, and every

thing" (II.i.626f.).  For Herod it is a world utterly lost when Marriam

dies, for he himself admits, "I have destroy'd the whole world"

(II.i.512).

This gloomy view of a world in deterioration is enforced by the

imagery.  As in Hamlet, here we find images of disease and rankness,[34] as well as numerous ones depicting the bestial aspects of men.  Herod

is described as an "angry boare" (I.i.17); he calls Animis a "silly

snaile" (I.iii.82); Salumith would have Alexandra run "dog-like backe,

and from the ground / Licke up the filth" she uttered (II.i.28f.).

Again Alexandra is called an "old hen" (II.i.95); and further images

liken characters to apes, owls, vipers, spiders, and flies.  The sug-

gestion is disturbing:  man is no longer distinguished by his nobility

and reason--attributes that have hitherto marked him as inferior only

to the angels.  He has now fallen below his intended station so that

he can hardly be discriminated from the most brutal and sordid forms

of life.

Also notable is a series of images which describe people as

buildings, in most cases subject to time and destruction.[35]  Augustus

says of Herod that "Rome hath power / To shake a stronger building"

(I.v.12f.).  Herod re-iterates the metaphor in saying that were Anthony

still alive, "my trunke should be the base / For his dread foes to build

ambition on" (I.v.49f.).  Antipater warns Animis:  "You fixe a ramme

to batter downe the life / Both of the King and kingdome" (I.ii.10f.).

Marriam tells Herod, "Y'ave dealt unjustly with me, and prophan'd / A

temple held you sacred" (II.i.228f.).  And Pheroas describes his mind

as "Like a decayed temple" (IV.i.103).

Against this background the figures of the play move, and as the

world is tainted, so are the inhabitants of it.  Nearly all of the

major characters exhibit some moral flaw.  Even the chaste Marriam,

although apotheosized in her death, is less than perfect amid the cor-

ruption of Herod's court.  She exchanges insults with Salumith and

Kiparim, and worse than this, she betrays her promise to Joseph when she confronts Herod with the secret command for her death. Marriam's transgressions, however, are small when compared to the rest of the characters'.

Among the women Salumith is especially villainous. She converts false evidence against Marriam into deadly accusations of guilt. She has no love or respect for her husband Joseph, whom she also ruins. Next she plots the death of her king and brother, and should she succeed in this she would perhaps then turn her venom against Antipater. "I've other plots in working," she tells him equivocally (III.i.338).

Alexandra is likewise selfish, so unnaturally so, that her character seems inconsistent.[36] Given the defiant portrait of her we have in the opening scenes (see especially II.i.203ff.), we can hardly accept her subsequent turning against Marriam to save her own life.

Among the men the same corruption is evident. Antipater and Herod are both accomplished in villainy. Pheroas, with no apparent motive, can be bought to belie Marriam. Even the minor figures, Animis and Niraleus, trick Antipater at the last when they arrest him; and also the comic characters--Lyme, Handsaw, Achitophel, Tryphon and the rest--all are easily manipulated in schemes of treachery. Only Joseph and the princes are free from blemish, but their goodness is feeble against the vicious powers that overcome them.

With the forces of evil so heavily outweighing the good, it is thus difficult to understand how at the end of the play satisfactory justice can be achieved. Yet, as we see, all of the villainous plotters, and chiefly Herod and Antipater, meet their deaths. Augustus, understandably awed by this, pronounces: "The gods have shewd their wonders" (V.ii.317). The statement is important, for it stands as the play's final attempt at theodicy.

Coming where it does, Augustus's attribution of the justice to Heaven can be taken, I believe, as the authors' view of the ultimate defeat of evil. Nevertheless, we are not convinced that we have seen the gods resolving the problems of men. But that such is the didactic intention of the playwrights seems clear, for throughout the action we are given hints of this coming resolution.

In a number of places the evil-doers are warned by other characters that Heaven's judgment awaits them. Alexandra tells Herod that "there's left / A hell to reckon with" (II.i.204f.). Soon afterwards Marriam adds, "Sir, take heed; / Vengeance is quicke in falling" (II.i.235f.). Next, when Joseph is slandered by Salumith, he cautions her, "Woman, looke up; / The vault of heaven is marble; this untruth / Will make it fall to kill thee" (II.i.289ff.). Herod's son Aristobulus, furthermore, advises him not to kill Marriam, "for th'account / Is heavy as damnation" (II.i.410f.). The two princes later warn Tryphon: "Villaine, speak truth, feare Judgement" (III.i.272). Pheroas, morose with his own guilt, prophesies that "a day / Will come, of Visitation, when the King / May wish these foule deeds undone" (III.i.353ff.).

There can be no mistake, therefore, that the playwrights' philosophy, in part at least, is that Providence controls the history of men.[37] Moreover, we realize that had the authors of Herod and Antipater worked out this scheme more effectively, they would surely have constructed a more powerful tragedy and one that resolved with more assurance the relationship of good and evil. Unfortunately, however, certain other factors in the play tend to obscure this important message since they ultimately muddle the theology.

The main flaw is an unnecessary mixing of divinities. Marriam and Joseph, because they are Jews, acknowledge the one God of Israel.[38] Herod, in contrast, because he is a Greek, decrees, "let no knee bow / But to the gods of Greece" (II.i.119f.). Later, nevertheless, he consecrates the rebuilt temple "Unto the God of Israel" (IV.ii.55). Antipater, who evidently believes in no god, still mentions Jove, Bacchus, Apollo, and Mercury (I.iii.336, 359). And finally, Augustus apparently thinks that the Roman gods "have shewd their wonders," since earlier in the play he has mentioned Jupiter (V.ii.263).

Still further confusions damage the framework of the play. Aside from frequent mentions of heaven and hell, we hear references to angels and devils, to the fact that Marriam dies like a "saint" (II.i.481), to the giants who threw mountains in the face of heaven, and we even see Antipater implore that he be made either a "god" or a "demi-god" (I.iii.360). Also, we hear about Furies and in fact see a couple of them. But the most perplexing aspects are the devilish visions of Antipater in the dumb shows, and the numerous ghosts that return from the dead. Are these real spirits from the other world, or are they only phantasms in the characters' minds?[39]

All of these elements, then, tend to undermine the significance of Augustus's final comment. The result is that we do not feel the power of Providence in control of history, and hence we regard the justice that takes place to be more the work of accident.[40] In fact, Antipater's downfall seems clearly to be just that, for he fails in

his evil not through any flaws in his plan nor through any power of
goodness in anyone else.  Herod simply happens to find out about
him.[41]

Nevertheless, the play cannot be counted as an artistic failure.  The lesson against ambition, illustrated in Antipater's career,
is still fairly effective.  He stakes all on his will, asserting that
his wits alone will bear him "'bove the true-borne" (I.ii.34).[42]  For
him "Power makes all things lawfull" (I.ii.35), and to gain this
power one needs only to act, since "Who can resolve, can doe" (I.iii.
375).  The trouble is that he is wrong, and though he nearly succeeds,
his evil in the end catches up with him.  Man's will is not totally
free, the play asserts; outside factors constantly thwart the plans
of men, be their intentions bad or good.  Alexandra and her son will
fly to Egypt, but they are caught.  Herod would like to kill both,
but he is forced instead to embrace them.  Augustus will "shower...
vengeance" on Herod (I.v.6), but he does not.  "To strike off these
my shackles," says a slave, "such a blow / I would give to my father"
(I.v.103f.).  But instead of freedom, this odious creature gains
only death.  Herod, moreover, blames his past murders on "Necessity"
(I.iii.26) and "Constraint" (I.iii.193); and there is doubtless some
truth in what he says.

The world of Herod and Antipater is finally one of little cer-
tainty.  Herod refers to the "darke of these confusions" (II.i.456).
A recurring image is of the weights which pull men down.  "What
plummets hang at vassals heeles," Herod exclaims (I.iii.86).  He
laments that Aristobulus, the High Priest, hangs "like a heavy
waight.../ Pressing our fortunes downeward" (I.iii.304f.).  Pheroas

feels "Sinne, like so many pullies hanging by, / To draw the soule still downward" (IV.i.31f.). In such a world, therefore, any move may be dangerous, so that to act in any way is also to gamble. "I've lost / All my delight at one throw," says Herod (II.i.458f.). "Kings," Antipater replies, "...must not play / At fast and loose" (II.i.463f.). In selling his poison Achitophel warns: "he that will purchase this, / Must pitch and pay" (III.i.417f.).

The final aspect to consider about the play's artistry is the characterization of the three title figures--Herod, Antipater, and Marriam.

Herod's characterization is perhaps the chief virtue of the play. Of the three major figures he is surely the most engaging. He is at once an appealing and a repugnant figure, while he shows a fairly convincing unity of character. That is, the varied aspects of Herod do not add up to be incompatible: they give him instead a complex but coherent identity.

We know from Hamlet's celebrated allusion (Hamlet, III.ii.16) what the traditional character of Herod had come to be like. The Herod familiar to the audiences of Shakespeare and of our play-wrights was of course the figure surviving from the medieval drama.[43] If this Herod had a favorite line from one appearance to the next, it was undoubtedly "Owt! owt! owt!"[44]

In this respect the present Herod begins in a familiar fashion. In his first scene, when he thinks that the High Priest and Alexandra have escaped, he rages and hisses in high style (I.iii.80ff.). His wrath is like that of the earlier Herod, who was similarly betrayed when the Magi failed to return:

ffy, losels and lyars! / lurdans ilkon!

Tratoures and well wars! / knafys, bot knyghtys none!

had ye bene woth youre eres / thus had thay not gone;

Gett I those land lepars / I breke ilka bone;

    ffyrst vengeance

Shall I se on thare bonys;

If ye byde in these wonys

I shall dyng you with stonys,

    yei, ditizance doutance.[45]

Yet, if the medieval Herod was quick to "fly out of his skin,"[46] his rage was nearly as quick usually to subside. Often in the mystery plays[47] all that Herod needed was a new scheme to "dyng" his enemies down. This would immediately restore his confidence and fill him with new delight.[48] Herod of Markham and Sampson shares this mercurial nature, for his anger diminishes suddenly. He has caught the High Priest and his mother in an act of treachery, yet he embraces them. He hotly condemns Marriam to death, but is instantly remorseful. Finally, he knows Antipater is guilty, yet he is moved to pardon him.

Still there are other ways in which the present Herod resembles his earlier counterpart. Both are masterful deceivers. The medieval Herod can rant furiously in front of the Magi when he hears that Christ will be king--but then convince them that he too wishes to go and worship![49] The present Herod deceives with such craft that his mother-in-law tells him, with fitting irony, "You can dissemble royally" (II.i.200).

Further, both Herods show extreme cruelty, rashness, and close-mindedness.[50] They also display a certain dependence on counsellors[51] and frequently lack good judgment. Both have a knack for bringing grief on themselves, and both seem in part to enjoy bewailing their woe.[52]

We soon find, however, that to extend this list of similarities becomes misleading. The truth is that the Herod of Markham and Sampson is markedly different from the older tyrant, primarily in his greater subtlety and sophistication.[53] He is a much quieter figure. He has none of the bombastic bluster of the medieval Herod and none of his boasting vanity. He does not rule entirely by threats and flattery,[54] nor does he brag of beating Magog and Madroke.[55] He takes no pride in the beauty of his face or clothing,[56] and he also speaks no French.[57] In short, he never tempts us to laugh at him.

The present Herod, nevertheless, is not reserved in nature either. His speech, for example, is often extravagant. It is pompous, yet attractively so; for Herod speaks with elevation and unmistakable power. His lines are often the most expressive and imaginative of the play since, like Richard II, Herod displays poetic sensitivity.[58] We also admire the flexibility of his diction--from the magnanimous command before leaving for Rhodes:

> if I have
> Power in your hearts, this day I challenge you
> To give them unto pastime, that the world
> May see, we dread not fortune...        (I.iii.269ff.),

to the frank confrontation with Antipater:

Sir, a word:

Y'are a faithlesse young man                          (II.i.244f.).

A further aspect of Herod's character is revealed in complement
with his sensitivity.  Herod is an actor and never misses a chance to
perform.  What is more, the postures he strikes are at times so convincing that we sense Herod himself being caught up in them.  Such
seems to be the case after the return from Rhodes.  When Salumith de-
fames Marriam, Herod is called on to restore her "poore forsaken
Vertue" (II.i.187).  His ardor is apt to the challenge, and just as
he reaches his full pitch of eloquence, his wife comes in.  The super-
latives he greets her with are impressive, but more remarkable is his
speech to Alexandra:

Nay weepe not Mother; come, I know your care,

And beare an equall burthen:  heere, O heere

Is the true tombe of Aristobulus                     (II.i.197ff.).

Coming from the man who has arranged the High Priest's death, this is
a strange statement.  But stranger still is the fact that Herod seems
to believe what he is saying--as surely as he later believes the evidence against Marriam.

Herod thus has a certain fascination about him because of the
defects he reveals.  We cannot forgive his mistakes, as we can, for
example, Lear's, even when he repents of them in his old age.  For
while Lear has been foolish, Herod has been brutal.  Yet we cannot
fail to care about Herod (his remorse is genuine), and in the final
scene it is him we favor and Antipater we condemn.

Antipater is unmistakably his father's son.  Like Herod, he is a
clever dissembler, and he is able to manipulate people with ease.  He

is a subtle villain who has extreme confidence. And because he resembles his father, he is more able than anyone else to see through
Herod and indeed remain always a step ahead of him. From the beginning it is Antipater who appreciates fully Herod's "Fine dissimulation!" (I.iii.16).

Notwithstanding our respect for Antipater, though, we have no
sympathy for him. To be sure, he has wit and shows faultless control
under pressure. The craft with which he lays his plans may occasionally match that of the most skillful villains, even Edmund and Iago,
and in fact he periodically reminds us of both of these.[59] And also
like these two, he fills us with fear and apprehension. His humor is
cynical--"My father shall be first, that order be observ'd" (I.iii.
385); his puns are threatening and frightful--"Thus sing we severall
descant on one plain-song, kill: / Foure parts in one, the meane excluded quite" (II.i.611f.). Antipater is, in short, chillingly evil.

In one important respect, however, the bastard son is unlike
his father. As we have seen, both Herod and Antipater are accomplished actors and can assume whatever rôle is needed for their pro-
tection. But never, like Herod, does Antipater obfuscate things. He
has full awareness at all times of his method and never fools himself
into assuming as real the false part he is playing. Watch him, for
instance, handle the accusation against the princes. Having forged
the letter himself, he reasons:

    If it be false, tis strangely counterfeit;
    The slave that did it had a cunning hand,
    And neere acquaintance with you: but, deare Sir,
    It shall be gracious in you to conceive

The best of these misfortunes:  who, that knowes

The world, knowes not her mischieves; and how slaves

Are ever casting mines up; for my part,

(Though there's no likelihood) I will suppose,

This is, and may be counterfeit                    (III.i.226ff.).

Antipater has reserve and knows the force of a "scurvy cold parenthesis" (III.i.256).  With no small relief do we watch his luck finally

run out.

Of Marriam there is little to be said.  Her rôle is so fleeting
that we catch only a glimpse of her before she is gone.  That she falls
victim to a cruel tyranny is pitiful, and that she answers her defamers
with silence is admirable.  Still, we feel no real sorrow at her death,
for we have never gotten to know her.

If anything, Marriam is puzzling.  Her love for Herod must be
unnatural if she can forget the deaths of her father and her grand-
father.  Even the murder of her brother seems far less upsetting to
her than we might expect.  Only when she hears the command threatening
her own life does she change her attitude--and then with surprising
suddenness.  Her love, she says, dies instantly and forever.  She
then confronts Herod boldly with the command and in so doing breaks
"all the bonds of chastity and truth" (I.iv.104) by which she has prom-
ised Joseph to remain silent.  Her rôle, therefore, is difficult to
interpret, as it must have been to write.  We can only wish that
Markham and Sampson had given us more insight into Marriam, for she
remains elusive.

## VI.  The History and Problems of Staging

Of the original productions of Herod and Antipater we know
nothing.  Only one statement survives, which is the advertisement
of the title page that the play "hath beene, of late, divers times
publiquely acted (with great applause) at the Red Bull, by the company
of his Maiesties Revels."  Furthermore, of this company few records ex-
ist.  G. F. Reynolds, in his history of the Red Bull theater, defines
the dates of the Revels as 1619-1623.[60]  The suggestion of Poynter
above, therefore, that the play was performed about 1621, cannot be
far wrong.

Regarding the staging of the play, we have only the text itself
to go on.  Aside from a fairly demanding list of properties--including
a rack, a scaffold, and the mysterious "banner full of ruptures"--the
requirements for the production seem not to have been unusual.  The
costumes need not have been lavish nor out of the ordinary from what
we believe to have been in the typical company's wardrobe.  As for
verisimilitude in dress, Reynolds observes that "Aristobulus's 'wastcoate'...is a significant reminder that historical accuracy was the
least of worries to the Elizabethan costumer " (op. cit., p. 176).

Unfortunately, no picture exists of the Red Bull as it looked
during the period of our interest.  Assuming, nevertheless, that the
text we have of Herod and Antipater is essentially the same as the
acting copy,[61] we can get some idea from it regarding the stage needed
for the performance.  Evidently the Red Bull playing area was like that
shown in DeWitt's sketch of the Swan, with one or two variations.

First, instead of two doors at the rear of the stage, the Red Bull may have had three.[62] The dumb show at the end of the second act (following 1. 637) suggests this fact when the army of the princes and that of Herod enter from opposite sides and then Augustus and the Romans enter "betweene them."

Moreover, a balcony seems to have been present, since in Act I, scene iv Antipater and Salumith observe the exchange between Joseph and Marriam from "aloft."

Finally, there seems also to have been some sort of discoverable space at the rear of the stage. While we have admittedly no proof for this, several scenes in the play point to the use of such a space, either a permanent alcove or an area concealed temporarily by a moveable curtain. As Reynolds suggests (p. 153), the "tribunal-throne," large enough to seat three actors, could be set in this area and left throughout most of the play. In the scenes where it was not needed, it would be hidden by the curtain rather than removed from the stage. Only once, in fact, might it be necessary to take the throne off of the rear stage. This would be in preparation for the scene in which Adda is tortured (IV.ii.), in which case the rack could be set up behind the curtain in place of the throne and then discovered.

The final scene of the play again suggests the presence of a rear stage, for here is an unusual instance in which the playing area represents two different locations at the same time. We see at once both Antipater in prison and Herod in the palace, and the characters move from one location to the other merely by going out one stage door and coming back in at another (Reynolds, p. 153). Assuming that the throne and rack have now been removed, we can imagine Antipater occupying the rear stage while Herod and his company utilize the front. That some of the ghosts should simultaneously haunt both Antipater and Herod may, of course, tend to destroy the illusion, but perhaps the striking effect of the double staging compensates for this flaw.

The scene, nonetheless, has not escaped criticism and has been termed "the least convincing part of the action."[63] Yet the author of this charge, A. C. Dunstan, objects not to the simultaneous setting but to the fact that Antipater should sleep out his excitement over the report of Herod's death. Certainly this is psychologically weak. It can perhaps be explained (if not excused) by noting the similarity between this scene and Act V, scene iii of Shakespeare's Richard III.[64] Clearly Markham and Sampson drew part of their inspiration here, though they hardly bettered the instruction.

### VII. The Original Text and the Present Edition

Herod and Antipater was entered in the Stationers' Register on February 22, 1622, and was printed that year by G. Eld for Mathew Rhodes. This was the only edition, although there may have been more than one issue.[65] Of the twenty-four copies of the play which are known to survive, four differ slightly from the rest in the first two leaves. The chief difference is that these four have on A2r an epistle signed by Sampson, whereas the majority of the copies have in place of this another epistle signed by Rhodes. Also, small variants in the type and setting of the title page distinguish these four copies from the others.[66] (See the reproductions of the title pages and epistles on pp. 1ff. below.)

In accounting for the differences W. W. Greg suggests that
Sampson's epistle "may have been an afterthought, or it may have been
the intention to restrict the dedication to a limited number of
copies."[67] Whatever the reason, the variants are insignificant since
they do not extend beyond the first two leaves. Neither Greg nor
Poynter has found any copy in which the text of the play, from A2v
onward, is not identical to that of the other copies. There are, however, four copies from which the first two critical leaves are missing,
and hence Poynter is forced to label these "unidentified." Yet these
also are said to be exactly the same as the rest, and it is therefore
reasonable to conclude that the play originally went through one edition only.[68]

In preparing the present edition I have followed the University
of Michigan microfilm copy for the text of the play. Where this copy
was illegible, due either to faulty inking or to damage, I have confirmed the reading by comparing the Folger and Huntington copies.
From the latter copy also I have borrowed the epistle by Sampson.
While my aim has not been to present a facsimile of the original text,
I have nonetheless made only minor changes. I have silently emended
what were clearly accidental errors, and I have also changed the cap-
italization, without notice, to conform to modern practice. In the
few cases of what seemed to be substantive errors in the original (for
example, lou'd where loud is needed), I have corrected the text and
given the quarto readings at the bottom of the page. Furthermore, I
have provided line numbers to the right of the text and added page numbers, while omitting the original page signatures, catchwords, and running title. For clarity, finally, I have added occasional information

(scene divisions, locations, stage directions, and punctuation)

in brackets.  I have not altered the lineation of the text, even

though the reader can often see how a re-division of the lines would

render more regular iambic pentameter.

*The true*

# TRAGEDY
## OF HEROD AND
### ANTIPATER:

*With the Death of faire Marriam.*

According to IOSEPHVS, the learned and famous *Iewe*.

*As it hath beene, of late, diuers times publiquely Acted*
(with great Applause) at the Red Bull, by the
Company of his Maiesties REVELS.

*Written by* { GERVASE MARKHAM,
*And*
WILLIAM SAMPSON. } *Gentlemen.*

## LONDON
Printed by G. ELD, for MATHEW RHODES, and are
to bee sold at his Shop at the vpper end of the Old
Bayly, neere *Newgate*. 1 6 2 2.

*The true*

# TRAGEDY

## OF HEROD AND

### ANTIPATER:

*With the Death of faire Marriam.*

According to I O S E P H V S, the
learned and famous *Iew*.

*As it hath beene, diuers times publiquely Acted*
(with great Applaufe) at the Red Bull, by the
Company of his Maiefties REVELS.

*Written by* {GERVASE MARKHAM, *And* WILLIAM SAMPSON.} *Gentlemen.*

*AT LONDON*
Printed by G. ELD, for MATHEVV RHODES, and
are to bee fold at his Shop at the vpper end of the Old
Bayly neere *Newgate*. 1622.

2

The Printers Epigrammaticall Epistle, to the understanding
Readers.


Readers:  whose hearts have sparkled with desire
To be inflamed with Promethian fire,
Fetcht from Pernassus shrine (the Muses mount)
To you I write, that make so deare account
Ev'n of arts meerest shadowes; you contemne                5
The drossy substance, highly priz'd by men
Of earthy breeding; who can never gleane
The least content from a true tragicke scoene
Of high and noble nature; nor care they
To heare, or understand; but see a play:                 10
For tragoedy or history, you shall
Never finde these at any stationers stall
Bestow one six-pence:  but, for bald discourses
Of commicke ribaldry, they'l draw their purses.
Hence is the cause, that stories (like to this)          15
Shall lie in darke obscurity, and misse
The printers presse, t'adorne and set them forth
In the true glories of their native worth;
When carrion-comedies (not worth an hayre)
Must be set out with <u>Excellent</u> and <u>Rare</u>;   20
Strange undeserving titles:  but, let these
Merit such liking as their readers please.
Heere I have sent and printed to your view,
A story, which I dare be bold is true;

Now newly writ, and truely worth your reading,                    25

Gather'd from learn'd Josephus:  all my pleading

Is, that it may your kinde acceptance gaine:

I then shall count my care, my cost, and paine,

  So happily bestow'd; that Ile be prest

  For your contentments, futurely to rest;                  30


                     Yours obsequious, in whats vertuous.


                            Math:   Rhodes.


[Epistle surviving in sixteen copies.  See pp. xxxi-xxxii above.]

To the right worshipfull, Sir Thomas Finch, Knight and Barronet,
and to all the most worthy and noble personages of that honourable
familie.

Worthy Sir; things of this nature, (as Cicero saith) defending
themselves, can offend none:  this poem, having freed it selfe
from detracting tongues and critticke censurers on the stage;
prostrates her selfe, with all that is hers, to your judicious
judgement.  And, indeed, to whom should I send her, but to him,     5
and those that ever lov'd her sacred Delphicke fires.  The
subject, though plaine, yet it is pithie; and, if we may give
credence to antiquity, it is nothing more then truth (as saith
Josephus) and, if in this any thing shall remaine that may relish
your pallate, as no quistion, but amongst beds of bryers there     10
may be one sweet rose; which, if from you it win applause, to
keepe it safe from the nipping of all busie brawling barkers,
curious caviliers, and all the factious family of Momus his mates:
I shal, as ever I have beene, so still rest, ever bound to your
worthinesse.                                                        15

Your Worships truly devoted,

William Sampson.

---

13.  caviliers) Quarto:  caniliers

[Variant epistle surviving in four copies.  See pp. xxxi-xxxii above.]

Herod, King of Judah.

Antipater, bastard son to Herod.

Alexander,
Aristobulus the younger, } sons to Herod and Marriam.

Pheroas, brother to Herod, and cup-bearer.

Joseph, brother-in-law to Herod, and husband to Salumith.

Aristobulus the elder, High Priest of Judah, son to

Alexandra, and brother to Marriam.

Archelaus,
Antipas, } grandsons to Herod.

Augustus, Emperor of Rome.

Decius,
Lucullus, } officers to Augustus.
Mutius,

Hillus, a centurion to Herod.

Animis,
Niraleus, } officers to Herod.

Tryphon, barber to Herod.

Achitophel, a drug-seller.

Disease, servant to Achitophel.

Lime, a mason.

Durt, a laborer.

Handsaw, a carpenter.

Marriam, Queen to Herod.

Alexandra, mother to Marriam.

Kiparim, mother to Herod.

Salumith, sister to Herod, and wife to Joseph.

Adda, wife to Pheroas.

Three Lords, two Slaves, a Eunuch, an Executioner, two Furies,
Attendants, Persons in the dumb shows, and Ghosts of Aristobulus
the elder, Alexandra, Alexander, Aristobulus the younger, Marriam,
Tryphon, Pheroas, Achitophel, Disease and Salumith.

Josephus, the Jewish historian, as chorus.]

The Prologue.


Times eldest daughter (Truth) presents our play;*

And, from forgotten monuments of clay,

Cals up th'heroicke spirits of old times,

Fam'd then as well for vertues as blacke crimes;

And with her owne tongue, and owne phrase, to tell          5

The actions they have done; or ill, or well.

Josephus th'ancient writer, with a pen

Lent by the Muses, gives new life to men;

Who breath'd such tragicke accents forth toth' eare

Of Hebrew armies, which you now shall heare;               10

Please you to sit attentive:  Wit hath runne

In a zodiacall circle, like the sunne,

Through all Invention; which is growne so poore

Shee can shew nought, but what has beene before:

Yet reverend History, which upon the stage                 15

Hath oft beene heard speake; hopes, even for her age,

Your strong hands will support her; shee must live

---

*For passages marked with an asterisk please see the
Notes of Explanation and Comparison beginning on p. 191.

---

12.  zodiacall) Quarto:  zodaicall    14.  has) Quarto:  ha's

Now by no heate, but what your beames doe give:

To gaine which (though her scoenes seeme grave and hie)

Shee heere and there with a loose wing doth flye; 20

Striving to make you merry: no other bayes

She reaches at, but this; your loves, your praise.

# THE TRUE TRAGEDY OF HEROD AND ANTIPATER.


## Actus 1. Scoena 1.

[Herod's palace at Jerusalem]


Enter at one dore Alexandra in her petticoate; at another,
Aristobulus the High Priest in his wastcoate or shirt,
both amazedly.


Qu. Alexandra.

O my thrice princely Sonne; thou hast forgot
That Time's our maister, and wee can dispose
But meerely of the instant.

Eld. Arist.

Madam true:

Nor have I lost a moment; yet I know,                            5
No diligence appeares to those, whose hearts
Doe both desire and waite.

Q. Alex.

Enough, enough;
Come let's away, my heart is wing'd with haste
That out-flies thought or motion; Aegypt (sweete)          10
Hath safety in it, not Jerusalem.

[I.i.]

Eld. Arist.

    I doe confesse it; yet this dangerous way

    Of our escape, hath many feares about it.

Q. Alex.

    There's pregnant reason for it, and our lives

    Are markes that Herod shoots at:* who but sees        15

    The wofull state of sad Jerusalem,

    And how this tyrant (like an angry boare)

    Roots up the goodly pines should cover him?*

    Hath he not slaine Antigonus,[1] destroyd

    Thy father and thy grandsire: (O my Lords,        20

    My deare lov'd Lords, my father and my husband;)

    Worthy Hircanus, noble Alexander;

    And at this instant lies hee not in waite

    For our destructions? Beldame that I am

    To prate at such a season; (holy sweete)        25

    Come let's away, our flight is so secure,

    No art can undermine it; any pause

    Opens our graves before us: flye, O flye.

Eld. Arist.

    I doe attend your Highnesse.

---

[1] For passages marked with Arabic numerals please see the Appendix
Concerning Sources beginning on p. 211.

[I.i. & ii.]

Q. Alex.

Harke, I heare                                                           30

The steps of some pursues us; prethee come,

Let Aegypt and not Juda be our tombe.                    Exeunt.


[Scoena 2.]


Enter at one dore Antipater [,] at another Animis, with a band

of soldiers.


Antip.

Is this the diligence your duty shewes,

To runne this slothfull pace?  By all I love,

Y'are worthy of blame in high termes.

Anim.

Princely Antipater.

Ant.

Y'are too improvident, and this neglect                  5

Will draw your life in hazard; understand,

Th'are lyons and not lambs you cope withall:

The Mother-Queene is subtile, and her sonne

Of high and noble spirit; should they scape,

You fixe a ramme to batter downe the life               10

Both of the King and kingdome.

Ani.                              Gracious Sir,

[I.ii.]

    Feare not my care; for nothing you can wish

    Is able to outstrip my diligence.

Antip.

    I but awake the duty which you owe

    Unto your King and countrey; when that moves,        15

    Children are strangers, fathers are unknowne,

    And where our Princes health is questioned,

    The lives we either borrow or doe lend*

    Must bee forgot and made ridiculous:

    You understand me, goe, dispatch, away.        20

Ani.

    With faith great as your longings.      Exit Animis & soldiers.

Ant.

    So, why so;

    Thus have I started bravely, and maintain'd

    My race with full speed to ambition;

    Much of my way is smoothed by the deaths        25

    Of proud Antigonus and Alexander,

    But chiefly of Hircanus, till hee went

    My torch could never kindle; could I now

    But dampe the High Priest Aristobulus,

    (As there's much water towards) and in it        30

    Drowne his old politique mother, halfe my way

    Lies as my thoughts would wish it; and how ere

    By birth I am a bastard,[2] yet my wit

[I.ii. & iii. ]

Shall beare me 'bove the true-borne;* for 'tis found,

Power makes all things lawfull, all things sound.                    Exit.


[Scoena 3. ]


Cornets:   and, enter Herod, Marriam, Kiparim, Alexander,

Aristobulus [the younger ], Salumith, Pheroas, Joseph and

attendants [and Antipater ].


Her.

Who sits on the tribunall, sits on thorne,

And dangers doe surround him; for at it

Envy stands ever gazing, and with darts

Headed with lightning strikes unto the heart

Of every noble action:  what can kings                              5

Doe, that the rude not censure and pervert

To vilde interpretations? Nay, although

Justice and mercy guard them; though mens faults

Are growne so odious, that even cruelty

Is a commended goodnesse, meere distrust                           10

A reasonable vertue; secrecie,

Important and most needfull; and suspect,

A worthy truth, which needs no witnesses:*

Yet, in this case, (where men cannot erre twice)

What shall we doe, that shall scape infamie?                       15

[I.iii.]

Ant.

    Fine dissimulation!

Her.

    O 'tis a hell to thinke on, that how ere

    Our natures are inclin'd to pitty, yet

    Our actions must be cruell (or so thought)

    To guard our lives from danger; wicked men         20

    With their sinnes so transforme us.  O my love,

    This unto thee I speake, whose tender heart

    I know hath bitter thoughts, when it records

    Thy fathers and thy grand-fathers mishaps:

    'Tis true, I caus'd them dye; but (gentle sweete)    25

    Necessity, thy safety, mine, nay all the lands,

    Were my most just assistants; and the act

    Was noble, how ere blam'd of cruelty.

Mar.

    My dearest Lord, doe not mistake my temper,

    My grand-father, and father, when they fell,      30

    How ever Nature taught mine eyes to weepe,

    Yet in my love to you I buried them;

    They were rich jewels once, but, set by you,

    They have nor price, nor lustre; 'tis mine eye

    That pitties them, my heart doth honour you.     35

Ant.

    O y'are a goodnesse past equality,

    And all the blessed times which are to come

[I. iii. ]

    Shall with more admiration then beleefe

    Receive th'incredible, but undoubted truth,

    Of your rare mildnesse, faith and temperance.         40

Her.

    It shall indeed; and be this kisse a seale

    Of our perpetuall love-knot; yet (my Queene)

    There are new treasons hatching, which (beleev't)

    Wil stretch thy patience higher:* Joseph, reade

    That strange and cunning letter.         45


               Joseph reads.


    I write short [, ] Alexandra, for feare of interception; that

    Herods cruelty extendeth to the death of thy husband, and im-

    prisonment of thy selfe, I lament:  ayd I cannot send thee;

    but if by flight thou canst escape, Aegypt shall receive thee:

    I am glad thy sonne Aristobulus is High Priest, let him     50

    accompany thy journey:  if I should deale for thee by force,

    I raise two mighty enemies, Rome and Juda; thou art wise,

    fare as my selfe:  Thine Cleopatra, Q. of Aegypt.[3]


Kip.

    These are miraculous treasons.

Sal.

    Subtile plots.         55

[I.iii.]

Phe.

    Strange interwinding mischiefes.

Mar.

    Say not so,

    Give them a gentler title; nothings read

    That doth accuse my mother or my brother.

P. Alex.[4]

    Indeed 'tis but an invitation                 60

    Of others love, not their confederacy.

Y. Ari.

    Th'Aegyptian Queen perswades, but their consent

    Is not conceived heere.

Her.

    Deere Wife and Sonnes,

    Love hath a blindfold judgement; would their hearts     65

    Were harmelesse as your wishes; but heere comes

    The man will reconcile us:  Captaine, speake,

    Where's Alexandra?  Where's Aristobulus?


    Enter Animis with soldiers, bringing two trunks.

Ani.

    Sir, they are fled.

------

56.  mischiefes.)  Quarto:  mischiefes,

[I.iii.]

Her.

    Fled! do not speake it; better thou hadst sunke        70

    To hell, then bring that mischiefe.

Antip.

    O the Divell!

    This was your hackney* pace.

Ani.

    By all that's true,

    I have not slackt a minute; they were gone        75

    Ere I had my commission, and so fast,

    My speed could not outstrip them; yet I tooke

    This luggage and their servants, whence (no doubt)

    Your Majesty may gather new instructions.

Her.

    Whence I may gather my despaire and griefe;        80

    Villaine, thou hast betray'd me; in their losse,

    I'm lost to fate and danger: silly* snaile;

    Could Sloth have crept so slowly? Why, thy way

    Was smooth as glasse, and thou mightst have surpriz'd

    Them easier then to speake it. O you gods,        85

    What plummets hang at vassals heeles; and how

    Doth sleepe and dulnesse ceaze them! But I vow,

    Thy life shall pay thy forfait.

---

82. and) Quarto: an

[I.iii.]

Ani.

    Gracious Sir:

Her.

    Talk'st thou of grace; and in this act hast lost,          90

    All things that's like, or neare it?  Did not scorne

    Hold me, my hand should kill thee.

P. Alex.

    Good Sir, thinke--

Her.

    That y'are too rude to offer thus to thrust

    'Twixt me and my resolution.

Antip.

                    Not a word;          95

    'Tis death t'outface this lightening.*

Her.

    Lost, and fled, and gone, and all my hope

    Turn'd topsie turvie downward?*  Joseph, harke.


    Herod whispers with Joseph, and beckens all the rest unto

    them, but Marriam, and Antipater.


Mar.

    Blest be the God of Juda, which hath brought

    My royall mother, and my brother safe,          100

    Out of the hands of sad captivity.

    O, I will offer sacrifice each day,

[I.iii.]

　　And make that houre a Sabbath, which doth bring

　　Them safe from threatning danger.

Antip.

　　　　　　　　　　　　Madam, amen;

　　With that prayer Ile joyne ever, and invoke　　　　　　105

　　Prosperity to guard them;--but (in heart)

　　Wish that damnation, like a thunder-bolt,

　　Would beat them into cynders.

Her.

　　　　　　　　　　　'Tis resolv'd,

　　Force shall compell what vertuously I would

　　Have sought from milde intreaty; for those trunks,　　　110

　　Goe throw them into Silo, let that lake

　　Devoure them and their treasures.

Jos.

　　　　　　　　　　　Not so good,

　　You may, by that meanes, blind-fold cast away

　　What you would after purchase with your blood;

　　But cannot then recall it: Sir, conceive;　　　　　115

　　There may be complots, letters, stratagems,

　　And things we cannot dreame of.

Kip.

　　　　　　　　　　Nay, perhaps

　　Some new negotiations.

[I.iii.]

Sal.

Paper tongues,

That may discover strange dissemblers.

Her.

True,

You have prevail'd, breake up those rotten tombes,                    120

Lets see what ghosts they harbor.  Ha, whats this?

Here they breake open the trunks, and finde Alexandra, and

Aristobulus the elder.[5]

Mar.

O me, my mother and my brother!  Eyes

Drop out and see not their destruction.

Antip.

Unhappy chance.

Jos.

Unfortunate young-man.

Y. Arist.

"Tis fate not to be shunned.                    125

P. Alex.

Woe the time,

Her.

What's heere:  The High Priest like a juggler?

Are these his holy garments; this his roabe,

His brest-plate and his ephod, his rich coate,

[I.iii.]

    His miter and his girdle?  Can it be,             130

    That this was once Queene of Jerusalem?[6]

    O you immortall gods, to what disguise

    Will treachery transforme us!

Q. Alex.

    Rather thinke,

    How sharpe a plague is Tyrannie:  O King,      135

    Remember 'tis the fiercest beast, of all

    That are accounted savage; yet delights

    In Flattery, which is the worst of them

    That are tame and domestique:  with these fiends

    My life can finde no pleasure; doe not then      140

    Blame me to seeke my freedome.

Eld. Arist.

    Mighty Sir,

    If life bee th'onely jewell Heaven can lend,

    And that in the Creation was not made

    A thing of equall purchase;* how can wee      145

    Offend, that but preserve it?  You may say,

    It hath deceiv'd us; yet Sir, I will thinke

    How ere it finish heere, 'tis but a stroke

    To draw it forth unto eternity.

Her.

    'Tis a good resolution; for (beleev't)      150

    Your dayes on earth are finisht; treacherous plots

    Like these, shall not ore take me.

[I.iii.]

Q. Alex.

But your tyrannie

Shall out-runne all example: Sir, Despaire

Armes me with truth and boldnesse; I dare now          155

Tell you, of kings, you are the wickedest;

And I, that in the ruines of my blood,

Read your destroying nature, and collect

Into a short briefe many tragedies,

Acted upon our family; what hope          160

Is left, that can assist us?

Her.

You are plaine.

Q. Alex.

Truth hath no need of figures: was't not you

That did betray Hircanus[7] in his flight

To the Arabian Monarch; and when laid          165

In harmlesse sleepe then slew him? Did not you

Hire the bloody Cassius to cut off

My fathers head, (the lov'd Antigonus?)[8]

Have you not kild my husband, troad my sonnes

Into the mire, that you might safely walke          170

Over their heads unto ambition?

And can you hope, that wee have any hope

In you, but desolation?

Her.

Your despaire

[I.iii.]

    Turne temperance into folly; charity

    Would more become the dying.

E. Arist.

                  Tis confest;           175

    Nor is it lost in this sad argument:

    We know our lives are forfeyt, take them Sir;

    To dye, is the first contract that was made

    Twixt mankinde and the world; tis a debt,

    For which there's no forgivenesse, th'onely cause    180

    For which we were created; and, indeed,

    To die's mans nature, not his punishment;

    What folly then would shun it?*  Boldly Sir,

    Use what your power hath conquer'd.

Her.

                  So I will;

    Your owne lips are your judges; and these hands,    185

    Arm'd with these two stillettoes at one blow,

    Shall thus drive all feares from me; but unite    Offers to stab,

    Two friends in mine imbraces; happy ones,    lets the poniard

    Exceeding happy ones; let not your feares    fal, & imbraces

    Draw to your eyes false figures, or make me    Ari. & Alex.

    Appeare that which I am not: come, I love you,    191

    Dearely I love you; all that I have done

    Constraint, and not my nature perfitted:

    Be henceforth free for ever; Aegypt, nor

    The world shall safelier guard you; as you stand    195

[I.iii.]

Thus shall you still support me; Holines          Places Arist. on

Upon my right hand;[9] Mother you shall sit          his right hand, and

Ever upon my left hand; both shall be          Q. Alex. on his left.

Mine armour, counsell, and prosperity.

Omnes.

This grace is past example; Herod's a god.          200

Her.

'Tis but their first step to felicity:

Antipater, your eare.


Herod whispers with Antipater, Antipater with Y. Alexander,

and Prince Aristobulus.


Y. Alex.*

Mother, the King is gracious.

Q. Alex.

Past beleefe,

Nor shall the memory lose* me; this not fain'd,          205

Ile fixe my prayers upon him.

Jos.

You shall doe

Wrong to your royall nature to suspect him.

E. Arist.

Sir, 'tis true;

I hold his word a rocke to build upon.

[I.iii.]

P. Arist.

    The sport is excellent, the wager firme,        210

    My person shall maintaine it.

Y. Alex.

    So shall mine.                            Clap hands.

Antip.

    And if I shrinke, make me a weather-cocke.

Her.

    How soone a foule day's cleered:  now to make

    Your happinesse more constant; Brother, know,      215

    The Temple of King Salomon which I

    The other day defaced and threw downe

    Low as the earth it stood on; once againe

    I will erect with double excellence.

    Joseph, my Brother, to your noble charge        220

    I give that holy building; see it fram'd

    To th'height of art and wonder; spare no gold,

    Jewels, nor rich imbosture;* I have mines,

    And all shall be exhausted; that the world

    May boast, King Herod out-went Salomon.       225

Jos.

    Sir, y'have ingag'd me where my heart desir'd;

    Doubt not my diligence.

Her.

                    Tis knowne too well:

[I.iii.]

    How now, what newes Centurion?  How stands fate     Enter Hillus.

    Betweene Augustus and Marke Anthony?

Hill.

    O royall Sir, deadly unfortunate;               230

    For, never was so sad a day before       Antip. [,] E. Arist. [,]

    Seene to ore-cover Aegypt:  to be briefe     Y. Ari. [,] P. Alex.

    Augustus hath the conquest; Anthony       whisper.

    Lies buried in the blood his warlike hand

    Strucke from his royall bosome; the sad Queene     235

    Oretakes him with like fury, and now both

    Are turnd to dust and ashes.

Her.

                   Thou hast spoke

    Much sorrow in a few words.

Hill.

                  But hold still

    Farre greater to unburthen:  soone as chance

    Had made Augustus happy, and orethrowne         240

    Faire Cleopatra, and her Anthony;

    Hee viewes his spoyles, and 'mongst them findes the aide

    Y'ad sent to interpose him:[10] now he frownes,

    Bends his inraged forehead, and protests,

    That Juda and Jerusalem shall curse          245

    They ever heard the name of Anthony:

    And this hee spake with such an emphasis,

[I.iii.]

    As shooke my heart within me; yet gave wings

    Unto my faith to tell you.

Her.

                  Sir, no more,

    Th'ast split me with thy thunder; I have made      250

    Rome and the world my mortall enemies;

    Yet vertue did transport me; but that guard

    Is no guard now:  tell me, Centurion,

    Where did you leave Augustus?

Hill.

                  Sir, in Rhodes.

Her.

    Tis a faire easie journey, I'm resolv'd;       255

    Nor shall perswasion change me; hence Ile goe,

    And as a hermite throw at Caesars feete

    My crowne and person;[11] if hee pitty them,

    My peace is made; if otherwise,

    My fault flies not beyond me.

Kip.

                  O my Sonne,      260

    This is a desperate hazard.

Sal.

                  Nay tis more;

    A tempting of your fortune.

Her.

                  Be content,

[I.iii.]

    Mother and Sister, nothing alters me;

    Nor doe they love me, that would draw my will

    To any other compasse:* Joseph, to you            265

    I leave the realmes protection,[12] and the care

    Of building up the Temple: nay, no teares,       The women

    They prophesie my death, which doe but shew    weepe.

    A low dejected countnance; if I have

    Power in your hearts, this day I challenge you     270

    To give them unto pastime, that the world

    May see, we dread not fortune.

Antip.

                  Tis resolv'd;

    And Ile be first to shew obedience.

    Sir, 'twixt my princely brothers and my selfe,

    I've made a match of swimming,[13] if you please    275

    But to allow the contract.

Her.

                How is't made?

Antip.

    That I and th'High Priest Aristobulus,

    Will swim more swift, more comely, and more wayes,

    Then can my princely brothers.

Her.

                Are all agreed?

[I.iii. ]

Eld Arist.

    All, if your Majesty consent thereto.             280

Her.

    For those young men it skils not; but Sir, you,

    I'm curious of your danger.

Ant.

                    There's no feare.

P. Alex.

    Tis a brave recreation.

Y. Arist.

              A fit skill

    For princes to delight in.

Eld. Arist.

                 Gracious Sir,

    Let me consort my brothers.

Her.

                 Be your will           285

    Your owne director; I am satisfied.

All.

    Why tis a match then.

Her.

    Yet looke well to your safeties; for my selfe,

    Rhodes is mine object: dearest love, farewell;

    This kisse seale my remembrance; Mothers, let     290

    Your onely prayers assist me; for the rest,

    Despaire not till my downfall; goe, away,

[I.iii.]

    Reply not, if you love me; only Antipater,       Exe. all but

    Stay and attend me further.  Princely youth,     Herod and Antip.

    Of all the hopes that doe attend my life,         295

    Thy greatnesse is my greatest; nor would I    Joseph returnes

    Imbarque me in this desperate vessell thus,    and listens.

    Wer't not to raise thy fortunes:  but tis now

    No time for courtship; onely, I must leave

    Two sad commandments with thee.

Ant.

              Speak them Sir,        300

    Without exception, you cannot devise

    While Ile not execute.

Her.

             Tis nobly said:

    Thou seest the High Priest Aristobulus,

    And knowst how like a heavy waight he hangs,

    Pressing our fortunes downeward, if hee live      305

    Our lives have no assurance.

Ant.

             Tis resolv'd,

    Hee never sees to morrow; soone at night, [14]

    When we doe swim our wager, Ile so teach

    His Holinesse to dive, that on the earth

    He nere shall tread to hurt us.

[I.iii.]

Her.

                                Thou hast hit           310

The object that I lookt at.

Jos.

                           (But shot wide

Of goodnes, and all good thoughts.)

Her.

                              This performd,

There yet remaines another thing to doe,

Which neerelier doth concerne me.

Ant.

                              Speake it Sir;

Your pleasure is mine armour.

Her.

                              Briefly thus,       315

If through my fortune, or Augustus wrath,

I perish in this journey; by that love,

Which nature, favour, or my best deserts

Can kindle in thy bosome; I conjure

And binde thee on the first intelligence,     320

By poyson, sword, or any violent meanes,

To kill my wife Marriam;[15] let no man

But Herod tast her sweetnesse; which perform'd,

My soule in death shall love thee.

Ant.

                              Thinke tis done;

[I.iii.]

    By Heaven the houre which tells me of your death,                    325

    Is th'oure of her destruction; I have sworne,

    And there's no fate can change me.

Her.

                                    Be thy selfe,

    Constant and unremoved; so farewell.

Jos.

    Two fiends like these were never spit from hell.[16]


    Exeunt Herod and Joseph severally.


Ant.

    Goe Herod, happy King; nay Herod, goe,                               330

    Unhappy, cause so happy; happy King,

    Whilst th'art a king; unhappy when no king:

    Hangs then mishap or hap upon a king, or no king?

    Then Herod, be no king; Antipater be King:

    And what's a king? a god: and what are gods, but kings?             335

    Jove, prince of gods, was petty King of paltry Creete;*

    Men subject are to kings and gods; but of the twaine,

    Their gods than kings commands, they rather disobay;

    Kings greater then; nay, better then, then gods:

    Then but a king or god, naught with Antipater;                      340

    And rather king then god; no god; a king, a king.

    When I complaine to Eccho but head-aking; it cries, a king:

    When I, in mirth, am musique making; it sounds, a king:

[I.iii.]

Each sight, when I am waking; presents a king:

When I my rest am taking; I see a king.                345

Last night I saw, or seem'd to see; nay, sure I saw

A crown hang ore my head; & through the crown a sword:

I saw, I sigh'd, I cryed, O when?  O when?

Fall crowne; yea fall with sword; fall both, so one may fall:*

But why dreame I of falling, that must rise;           350

Nay runne, nay leape, nay flie unto a crowne?

Gyants heape hills on hills, to scale high heaven;*

I, heads on heads, to climbe a kingdomes skye:

But oh, I am a sonne; a sunne, O happy name;

A sunne must shine alone, obscuring moone, and starres:  355

I, but I am a bastard; what of that?

Men base by birth, in worth are seldome base;

And Natures out-casts, still are Fortunes darlings:

Bacchus, Apollo, Mercury; bastards, yet bravest gods:*

Then, why not I a god, a demi-god, or worthy?*         360

You gods, you demi-gods, you worthies then assist me;

That, as our birth was like, our worth may beare like price:

If they refuse; come devils, and befriend me;

My breast lies open; come; come Furies and possesse it;

Hatch heere some monstrous brood, worthy of you and me;  365

Which all posterities may know, but none beleeve;*

Whereat the sunne may not goe backe, as once it did,

At Atreus tyrannie;* but fall and dye for ever:

Wherat the heav'ns may quake, hell blush, & Nature tremble;

[I.iii.]

And men (halfe mad) may stand amaz'd.*  So, so, it works, it works;

My breast swels to a mountaine; and I breed                    371

A monster, past description; to whose birth,*

Come Furies, and bee mid-wives. Harke! O harke!


                    Dumbe shew.

Musique:  and, enter Egystus and Clitemnestra dancing a curranto,*

which is broken off by the sound of trumpets:  then, enter

Agamemnon, and divers noblemen in triumph:  Egystus whispers with

Clitemnestra, and delivers her a sleevelesse shirt; then slips

aside:  Clitemnestra imbraces Agamemnon, he dismisses his traine;

shee offers him the shirt, he offers to put it on,  and being in-

tangled, Egystus and she kils him; then departs, leaving at

Antipaters feete two scrowles of paper.

Ant.

So shall it be; shall it?  no shalls; tis done, dispatcht:

Who can resolve, can doe; who can dispose, can better:          375

My way, seaven single persons, and two houses crosse;*

Supported by a many headed beast:

O, had they all one head, or all their heads one necke,

Or all their necks one body, which one blow might broach;*

But had they Hydra's heads, Gerions bodies; Hercules,          380

By making them away, would make his way to heaven:

But as an hunger-starved* tyger, betweene two heifers,

Here yawnes, there gapes, in doubt where first to fasten;*

So doubt I where to set my pawes, but care not where;

[I.iii.]

My father shall be first, that order be observ'd;*                    385

Whose death I wish, not worke, lest piety be wanting;

Rome will I hope ease me of that disturbance:

Herod is come Augustus, friend to thy foe, and so thy foe;

Keep him Augustus, nay kill him Augustus, or Jove kill him & thee;

Passe he by land or sea, or hell, or under heaven:                    390

O earth; food unto him, or none, or noysome give:

O sea; his ships or sinke in sands, or drinke in waves:

O heaven; or stop his breath, or lend contagious breath:

O hell; for kindnesse, call him in thy wombe:  in summe,

Gape earth, swell seas, fall heaven, hell swallow him:                395

But, let me see; what say my hellish counsellors?

Egystus wooes, and winnes, and weares a crowne:  a queene

Receives with love (false love) the victor king; unarm'd,

She cloaths him in her handi-worke, a shirt,

Which had no head or armes to issue out;                              400

Intangled thus they slew him:  let me see,

What have they left?  thus Clitemnestra writes;

Per scelera semper sceleribus tutum est iter;*

Fond is the stay of sinne; sinne safest way to sinne;

Egystus leaves this axiome;                                           405

Nec regna scotium ferre, nec tedae sciunt;*

None, or alone; kings can indure no rivals;

I understand you well; and so will worke;

Whetting against my father both his wife,

His sister and her husband; some by feare,                            410

[I.iii. & iv.]

    Some by beleefe, and some by jealousie:

    Thus rise I on their heads, and with their hands

    Rip up their naturall bowels:  tis decreed,*

    The plot is laid, parts must bee playd,

    No time delaid.*                         Exit.          415


[Scoena 4.]


Enter Lime the mason, Handsaw the carpenter, and Durt the
labourer.


Han.

    Tis a good handsome plot,* and full of art;

    But how like you my modell for the timber-worke?

Lim.

    Pretty, pretty, if the seates be not too spacious.

Dur.

    O, tis much the better, and fitter for the Scribes &

    Pharisies to sleepe upon:  but here comes the Lord Joseph.     5


Enter Joseph.


Jos.

    Well said my maisters, and how mounteth the brave Temple?

    may a man stand on the top of it and orelooke

    the sunne?

[I.iv.]

Han.

 The sunne is very high Sir; yet there is never an

 almanacke-maker, but may lie on his backe and behold   10

 Capricorne.

Jos.

 Tut, any foolish citizen may doe that which hath

 his wife for his maister: but stay; what's hee?


 Enter Achitophel & Disease, with a banner full of ruptures.*


Ach.

 Come away Disease, and hang up these my trophees,*

 whilst I with gentle ayre, beat upon the eares of passengers.

Dis.

 At hand Sir, and heere is your ensigne; as for your   16

 drugges, there is not one of them but is able to send a man

 to God or the Divell in an instant.


    Achitophel sings.


Ach.

 Come will you buy, for I have heere

 The rarest gummes that ever were;   20

 Gold is but drosse and features dye,

 Els Aesculapius tels a lie:

    But I,

[I.iv.]

  Come will you buy,

 Have medicines for that maladie.        25

Jos.

 What's hee?

Lim.

 O Sir, it is one that undertakes to know more simples,

 then ever grew in Paradise; tis Rabbi Achitophel.

Jos.

 What, the famous mountebanke?

Dur.

 The same Sir.             30


     Achitophel sings.


Ach.

 Is there a lady in this place,

 Would not bee mask't, but for her face;*

 O doe not blush, for heere is that

 Will make your pale cheekes plumpe and fat.

   Then why          35

    Should I thus crye,

 And none a scruple of mee buye.

Jos.

 Reverend Jew; I heare y'are fam'd for many rarities;

 As sculpture, painting,* and the setting forth

[I. iv.]

Of many things that are inscrutable; 40

Besides you are a learned rare physitian.

Ach.

I know as much as ere Sambashaw* did,

that was old Adams schoolmaister; for, look you Sir: Sings.

Heere is a rare mercurian pill,

An anodine helps every ill; 45

The dissenterea, and the gout,

And cures the sniveling in the snout.

The sicke,

Or any cricke,

Straight cures this diaphoreticke. 50

Jos.

I shall have imployment for you.

Ach.

The Jew is all your creature, and his skill

Hee'l willingly bestow upon your goodnesse.

Jos.

O Sir, you shall not.

Dis.

Yes Sir, my maister will willingly give you his skill; 55

Yet, with this memorandum, you must pay for his good will.

Jos.

I am no niggard, Sir.

Dis.

Besides, my Lord, there's never a pibble in Jordan, but

my maister is able to make the philosophers stone of it.

[I.iv. ]

Dur.

    O wonderfull! as how I pray you Sir?                  60

Dis.

    Why by extraction, solution, reverberation, coagulation,

    fixation, vivivication, mortification, & multa alia.

Ach.

    Peace knave, I say, these pearls must not feed porkets.

Han.

    How, doe you make swine of us?* I tell you we are

    as arrand* Jewes as your selfe.                   65

Jos.

    No more, y'are all for mine imployment; you for stone,

    You for painting, you for timber-worke;

    No man shall want his merit:  goe, away,

    Apply your labours, there's a largesse for you.

All.

    O brave Lord Joseph.                          70


                         [Achitophel] Sings.


Ach.

    Come to me gallants you whose need,

    The common surgeons cannot reede;

    Heere is a balme will cure all sores,

    Got in broyles, or unwholsome whores.

          Come away,                          75

[I.iv]

For why the day,

Is past, and heere I cannot stay.                    Exe. all but Joseph.


Enter Alexandra & Marriam, Antipater & Salumith aloft.


Q. Alex.

O cease my Marriam, teares can doe no good;

This murder's past example;[17] to be drownd,

Drownd in a shallow murmure where the stones                80

Chid the faint water for not covering them.*

O, 'twas a plot beyond the Divell sure;

Man could not have that mallice.

Mar.

Madam yes,

And 'twas some great one too that had his fist

Thrust in the blood of Aristobulus.                          85

Q. Ale.

For which blood Ile have vengeance, & my tears

Shall never drye till it bee perfited.

Jos.

Madam, forbeare complaining; would this were

The worst of mischiefes journey.

Mar.

Know you worse?

[I.iv]

Jos.

    I dare not speake my knowledge, though my heart       90

    Leapes twixt my lips to utter mysteries.

Antip.

    Note you that Salumith?

Sal.

    Yes, it hath pincht her on the petticoate.

Mar.

    Sir, as y'are noble, whatsoere you know

    Of these mishaps, with freedome utter it.

Q. Al.

                                  Utter it;       95

    For Heav'ns sake utter it, noble, worthy Lord.

Jos.

    Madam, I dare not.

Mar.

    As you love vertue speake it; let my teares

    Winne so much from thy goodnesse; noble Sir,

    Soule of thy generation, thou honestest 'mongst men:    100

    O speake it, speake it.

Ant.

                    Note you this courtship?

Sal.

    Yes, tis sorcery.

---

93. Yes,) Quarto: Yes.

[I.iv.]

Q. Alex.

    Good sweete, unlocke these counsels.

Mar.

    By all the bonds of chastity and truth,

    It shall proceede no further.

Jos.

                    You have laid         105

Such strong commandments on me I must yeeld:[18]

    Harke, your eares.                         Whispers.

Antip.

    Are they not kissing Madam?

Sal.

    Yes; may poyson flow betweene them.

Q. Alex.

    Antipater; he drowne him!                 110

Jos.

    Nay, be still; you shall heare greater mischiefe.   [Whispers

Mar.                                            again.]

    Poyson me, if he perish!  O you gods,

    What treason lurkes in greatnesse; this hath made

    Wounds in my heart, through which his love and name,

    Is fled from me for ever!

Jos.

                    Tis a fault          115

Which asks your deepest wisedome:  come, let's in;

Ile tell you stranger stories.

[I.iv. & v.]

Q. Alex.

                    Yet I feare,

    None that can draw more vengeance or despaire.          Exeunt.

Antip.

    Awaken Madam, they are vanished.

Sal.

    Not from mine outrage, that shall like a storme          120

    Follow them and confound them;*[19] I will make

    The world in blood, text* downe my crueltie.

Ant.

    I cannot blame you, tis strange impudence.

Sal.

    Ile be reveng'd; by all my hopes I will,

    Highly and deeply; shallow foole, no more;              125

    Still waters drowne, the shallow doe but roare.        Exit Sal.

Ant.

    Ile not be farre behinde, but helpe to send

    All unto hell; tis for a crowne I stand,

    And crownes are oft the ruines of a land.             Ex. Ant.


                    [Scoena 5:  Rhodes]


    Enter Augustus, Decius, Lucullus, and attendants.


Aug.

    Thus have we queld rebellion; thus (like smoke)

[I.v.]

    Vanishes hence the name of Anthony:

    Only some props remaine yet; which Ile rend

    Up by the roots and scatter:  amongst which

    Ungratefull Herod is a principall;           5

    On whom Ile shower my vengeance.        Enter Mutius.

Mut.

    Gracious Sir; the King of Juda, like a supplicant,

    Desires accesse unto your Majestie.

Aug.

                      Who, Herod?

Mut.

    Sir, the same.

Aug.

            Tis a strange over-daring.

Luc.

    An attempt wisedome would hardly runne to.       10

Aug.

    Call him in;

    Hee dares not come to brave us; Rome hath power

    To shake a stronger building; and his feares

    Are glasses of his danger:  no man looke

    On Juda, but with hatred.        Enter Herod.     15

Her.

    Mighty Sir; to you, as him of whom I first receiv'd

---

16.  receiv'd) Quarto:  receiv'd.

[I.v.]

The crowne of Juda, humbly I returne it;[20]

And thus arise.  Know now (the great'st 'mongst men)

Tis not for life I plead, but honesty,

For vertue, valour, honour, prowesse, grace,                    20

And all good mens acquaintance:  I confesse,

I ayded Anthony; if for that I fall,

A true friends teares shall bee my funerall.

Luc.

Tis a rare gratulation.

Dec.

       I'm affraid

New feare will alter it.

Mut.

       Observe the Emperour.                    25

Her.

Tis true (great Sir) your sacred hand was first

Invested mee in Juda; gave mee that

I can forsake with comfort:  keepe it still;

Who from a crowne is rid, is free from cares;*

I prize the worth, lesse then two fluxine* teares.              30

Aug.

This is a kinde of braving.

Her.

       Heare me forth;

And when y'ave heard; this, for extremitie:

Since first the time I wore the sorrowfull wreath,

[I.v. ]

(For crownes and sorrowes are incorporate,

And hang like linkes, one wreathed in another)          35

Since first the crowne I wore, you knew my grieves;

But nere reliev'd me by person or by deputy;

No, not when Asia and the Affricke strands[21]

Joyn'd both to over-throw me:  onely, then

The ever-prais'd (now lost) Marke Anthony          40

Thrust forth his hand and staid me; he kept firme

My foote that then was sliding; I, for this,

Sent him not ayde, but rent long purchased.

O (gracious Sir) view mine oblidgements well,

And you shall see vertue did governe me.          45

Why, did his life yet lie within my hands,

Thus would I straddle ore him as I stand;

Mine armes dissever'd like two Rhodian props;

And ere I bent, my trunke should be the base

For his dread foes to build ambition on:          50

This would I doe; and, if this bee a crime,

It is so good an one, I scorne my breath:

Who lives the lives the longest still must end in death;

And so must I.

Aug.

Thou art thine owne judge Herod:  call a slave,          55

A desperate slave; 'mongst all our prisoners,          Exit Mut.

Chuse him that hath least mercy:  you shall finde,

Your friendship had a false grownd.[22]          Enter Mut. & a slave.

[I.v.]

Her.

    Caesar, no; vertue was the foundation, and you may

    Batter, but not orethrow it.

Aug.

                       Well Ile try                60

    The utmost of your fortitude:  arme that slave;

    And sirrah, kill that traytor; tis a worke

    That brings you home your freedome.

1. Sla.

    Gracious Sir, what is he I must murder?

Aug.

    Tis a king.

1. Sla.

                  Ha!                           65

Dec.

    Villaine, why star'st thou?  Strike, I say, you slave.

1. Sl.

    Slave, Ile not strike; knowst thou or he, or he, or Caesar

    What tis to bee a murderer; nay, more,

    The murderer of a king; nay, most of all,

    To murder God himselfe; (for such are kings:)        70

    O you dull bloody Romans; see, in's eyes

    Are thousands of arm'd arm'd angels; and each ray

    A flame of lightning ready to devoure

    The hand thats lift gainst sacred majesty.

    Caesar, I'm no Italian; though thy slave,          75

[I.v.]

    I will not be thy divell; those are bred

    Ith'shambles, let them butcher; fetch for this

    Some from the Roman gallowes; for they are

    Hangmen that must performe it; and thou lookst

    Like one:  goe, take the office, Ile not doo it.        80

Aug.

    The slave's affraid to strike him; timerous coward:

    Call another.                     Exit Mutius.

1. Sla.

    Timerous!  Caesar, no:

    Were I to scale a tower, or sacke a towne,

    I'de doo't; although the ruines fell like quarries on me:    85

    Timerous!  I neare fear'd mankinde; Caesar, know,

    Nor earth nor hell hath ought that can affright me:

    I've buckled with proud Julius thine uncle, and was one

    That, by expulsion, beate him from bright Albion:

    And yet to kill a king, I'm timerous.*        Ent. Mut. & 2. Sla.

Aug.

    Let that slave have the weapon:  sirrah, kill        91

    That king, and have thy freedome:  wilt thou doo't?

2. Sla.

    Yes, for my liberty,

    As soone as you can speake it:  shall I strike?

Aug.

    Stay, what's thy country?                95

[I.v.]

2. Sla.

    Rome, Rome; I was bred in one of those colledges

    where letchery and murder are pue-mates:  come, will

    you give the word?

Her.

                Doe not deferre it Caesar,

    I have made peace with my conscience long since.

Aug.

    Why then strike.                                    100

    Yet villaine hold; art not amaz'd to doo't?

2. Sla.

    Amaz'd, why?

    To strike off these my shackles, such a blow

    I would give to my father.

Aug.

                      But a worse

    Shall fall upon thy carcasse:  binde that slave,        105

    And throw him headlong downe into the sea;

    The earth's too much infected.  --Herod, thus

    Mine armes gives thee thy freedome:  take thy crowne;

    Weare it with safety; and but be to mee

    Faithfull; Ile love thee as did Anthony.           110

Her.

    Caesar is royall; and, by this, hath bound

    A faithfull servant to him.

[I.v. & II.i.]

Aug.

                    For that wretch,

Give him his liberty; since th'ast serv'd

Vertue, thou shalt serve Caesar; henceforth be

Commander ore a legion:  those that know          115

Goodnesse; by goodnesse ever greater grow.

1. Sla.

Caesar's a god in all things.           Exeunt omnes.


                   Finis actus primae.*

---

                  Act. 2. Scoena 1.

             [Herod's palace at Jerusalem]


Enter at one dore Marriam and Alexandra; at another

Kiparim and Salumith, they meete and passe disdainfully.[23]


Kip.

Lord how their poyson swels them.

Sal.

Sure they'l burst, if this strong chollicke hold them.

Mar.

Mother, withdraw; the Greeke[24] begins to scold.

[II.i.]

Sal.

    And why to scold, proud Madame?

Mar.

    Nay, I want a tongue for your encounter.          5

Kip.

    Yet this thing,

    Of which thou art derived, ought to know

    Shee owes me some obeysance; though she was

    Mother to him that wore the crowne,[25] I am

    Mother to him that weares it.          10

Sal.

    Tut, pride loves not to distinguish:  goodly Lord,

    not so much as how doe you forsooth; (every foolish citizens

    salutation;) nor haile to the sister of my Lord the King,

    (every court-coxecombes congee;) nor save you sweet

    Lady, (fooles and physitians orizons) [.]          15

Mar.

    How this shewes.

Kip.

    It shewes that you are insolent.

Q. Alex.

    Insolent:  hugge it sweetly, tis your owne;*

    And every sinne besides that's damnable:

    Come, y'are despised Grecians; so prophane,          20

    Ignoble and unholy, that our tribes

    Are staind in your conjunctions; poore things, know,

[II.i.]

Your titular King, in whom your glories dwell,

Is but a royall murderer; your selves,

And his proud bastard, bloody substitutes:                    25

O, I could paint you bravely; for my grieves

Have all your perfect colours.

Sal.

                              Come I could

Make you runne dog-like backe, and from the ground

Licke up the filth you utterd.*

Mar.

                              Never sure;

Sheele leave it where she found it.

Sal.

                              Yes, and you            30

Leave vertue where you found it; harke you Queene,

You are unchast, and most incontinent.

Mar.

Incontinent:  with whom?

Sal.

His picture lies within you; plucke it out,

And let your false heart follow.                              35

Mar.

It is Truths part to suffer; so must I.

Sal.

Vengeance upon such sufferance.

[II.i.]

Q. Alex.

Come, y'are a barbarous creature.

Kip.

Base Edomite.[26]

Q. Alex.

                    Slanderous Grecian.

Sal.

Old beldame.

Q. Alex.

            Young cocatrice.                                    40

Kip.

S'death, I could teare thine eyes out.              Enter Antip.

Q. Alex.

Do but (this)* that motion shall destroy thee.

Sal.

Marry mew.

Ant.

Hold in the name of vertue; heere's a braule

Able to inflame patience:  beautious Queene,              45

Divinest Alexandra; what can move

These stormes in this calme weather.

Mar.

                              Flattering Sir,

You best can close up mischiefe.

———————

44. vertue) Quarto:  verue

[II.i. ]

Ant.

                                If I may,

Ile lay my life a subject to your mercies;

Make me your footstooles to appease your wrathes;        50

My blood Ile make your sacrifice.

Q. Alex.

                                  No more;

I that but now shed teares, now laugh: O God!

To see so brave a maister-piece of villany

By such a bastard issue bee compacted:

Thou make attonement?  Hence bastard, hence;        55

The dregges of lust, the foule disease of wine,

That wert begot when sinne was revelling:

Thou make attonement?  No; goe learne to drowne

The Lords elected people; heere stands shee

That lookes to tast thy poyson.

Ant.

                                  Miracles!        60

Wrest not my good thoughts (Madam) for I call

Just Heaven to witnesse how I lov'd your sonne;

And would my selfe have dyed to ransome him;

But your misprision* I impute to heate

And chollericke spleene, which now misgovernes you.        65

Kip.

Nay, you should thanke her for abusing you;

Wee are become her vassals.

[II.i.]

Ant.

                    Thinke not so.

Sal.

    Yes, and cry vengeance for it; wicked one,

    There's wier whips in making, and I know

    Furies will soundly lash you; you, and you;         70

    Both are markt out to perish; faith you are.    Enter Joseph.

Jos.

    How now; what means this outrage?  Peace for shame;

    This talke fits stewes and brothels:  come, no more;

    Mother, your judgement should be farre more wise;

    And Madam, you should be more temperate:         75

    At princes hands, all injuries should looke

    Not for revenge but patience.

Kip.

    Thou which art made of cowardise and feare;

    Dost thou confirme their actions?

Sal.

                    Yes, tis fit;

    Lust still must flatter falshood.         80

Jos.

    Ha; what's that? why Wife--

Sal.

    Call me not Wife;

    The sound of death hath farre more musique in it:

    Wife? O, my fate! Wife unto such a letcher?

[II.i. ]

Jos.

   Why Salumith.                                         85

Sal.

   Ile be no Salumith of thine, there's your love;

   She whom you foster in her insolencies;

   Shee's your Salumith:   O crudulous* women,

   How easily are you guld, with a seducing kisse!

Ant.

   Now it workes.                                     90

Sal.

   A faire word makes the Divell seeme a saint;

   But Ile be reveng'd, and in so strange a course

   As never woman tooke.   D'yee perpetrate* my goodnes?

   There's your Salumith.

Ant.

                  Admirable still.

Kip.

   And there's th'old hen her mother,               95

   A couple of season'd dishes, fall too, fall too.

Ant.

   Nay Madam, y'are too bitter.

Jos.

   By Heaven & happines, I know not what this meanes;

   Yet were the King not sodainly return'd,

--------

86.   there's) Quarto:   ther'es

[II.i.]

    And crav'd our swift attendance; I would sift            100

    And try this language strangely.

Ant.

    Is the King return'd?

Jos.

                        He is, and safely.

Kip.

    Then my hate, Ile give thee fire to worke on.

Sal.

    So will I; I'm arm'd with able mischiefe.

Ant.

    And my plots                                   105

    Shall runne as fast to ayd and second you.

Jos.

    Ladies, shake hands with passion, and let's joyne

    To meete the King with royall cheerefulnesse.

Mar.

    Sir, not I;

    Let them that love their horror seeke it still:         110

    Goodnesse I want, with him is all thats ill.

Q. Alex.

    You may report our speeches; say, our joy

    Is, we have left no more he can destroy.       Exe. Q. Alex.

Jos.                                    & Marriam.

    This is a violent passion.

[II.i.]

Ant.

Let it rule;                                                    115

Repentance needes must follow.


Enter Herod, P. Alex. [,] Y. Aristob. [,] Pheroas, and
attendants.


Omnes.

Welcome, O welcome to Jerusalem;

May Herod live for ever fortunate.

Her.

We thank you:  Mother & Sister, rise; let no knee bow

But to the gods of Greece; by whose support            120

Wee stand unshakt and unremoov'd:  but (me thinkes)

In this great universall rhapsodie*

Of comfort and amazement, I doe misse

Two faire companions of my happinesse:

Where is my lovely Marriam?  what withdrawes          125

Her mother Alexandra?  Sure, my heart

Lookt for their entertainment.

Jos.

                              Gracious Sir,

Th'unfortunate destruction of her sonne,

The High Priest Aristobulus (late drownd

Within the river Rigall)[27] so takes up                130

[II.i.]

    Their hearts with powerfull sorrow, that their minds

    Are borne with nothing but calamity.

Her.

    That guest is soone removed; goe, my Sonnes,

    Informe your grandmother and mother-queene,

    How much I long to see them.

P. Alex.

                      Tis a worke            135

    Worthy our duties.

Her.

                  Joseph, goe, attend;

    There's need of your assistance.          Ex. P. Alex. [,]

Sal.                         Y. Ari.[,] & Jos.

    Yes; and all I feare too weake to draw them:

    Royall Sir, you are abus'd in your credulity;

    It is not griefe but malice, bitter spleene,        140

    An anger I may call treason, which keepes backe

    These two from noble duties:  Sir, they say

    You doe usurpe, and are a murderer,

    And teach all yours to murder; that you are

    No lawfull King of Israel; but a Greeke        145

    Descended basely; drawne from polluted blood:

    Prophane, unholy; nay, (indeed) what not

    That Rancor can imagine?  Sir, I feare

---

134.  mother-queene,) Quarto:  mother-queene,,

[II.i.]

   Your life is plotted on; a wrath like theirs,

   So lowd, so publique, nay so impudent;           150

   Is not without assistance.

Ant.

                      Bravely urg'd.

Her.

   Good Sister, thinke not so; a losse like theirs

   Will make dumbe patience muteny; beleev't,

   It moves much in my owne brest; as for plots,

   Alas, what can they dreame of?

Sal.

                    Desperate things.       155

   Things which may shake your foot-hold; for, I feare

   The Queene is turnd an aspis, and will spread

   Her fatall poyson ore you; if you doate,

   The lethargie will kill you:  Sir, tis said,

   Nay, t'will be prov'd she is incontinent.       160

Her.

   Incontinent!  with whom?

Sal.

   With him I blush to mention; Joseph Sir,

   Joseph my husband wrongs you.

Her.

                    Peace for shame;

   Your jealousie doth foole you.[28]

[II.i.]

Kip.

                    Well, take heede

Affection doe not blinde you:  tis a staine,          165

Almost the whole world finds out; and a truth,

Not hidden, but apparant; pray you Sir,

Speake you what is reported.

Ant.

                    Tis not fit,

Nor dare I credit Rumor, chiefly when

It speakes of such great persons; yet tis true,      170

Many vilde things are utterd; nay indeed

Some prov'd I wish were hidden:  but alas,

Who knowes not Slander's ever impudent?

Sal.

Doe not give truth that title; for you know,

It will be prov'd by many witnesses.                 175

Her.

Thart jealous Sister, and than such a fiend,

There is no worse companion:  come, no more;

Should all the prophets, patriarchs, and priests

Lodg'd in the holy bookes of Israel

Come forth and tell this message, I would stand      180

Boldly and interpose them;* for I know,

There is no truth to guard them; no nor faith.

O my divinest Marriam, how art thou

And thy great sweetnesse injur'd?  Th'unblowne rose,

[II.i.]

The mines of chrystall, nor the diamond,                                    185

Are halfe so chast, so pure and innocent.

O poore forsaken Vertue, how art thou

Torne downe by thy despisers, and consum'd

By th'envious flame of the malicious?

But I am come to guard thee, and restore                                    190

Thy goodnesse backe with interest; for I vow

To heare naught but thy praises:  heere shee comes;


Enter P. Alex. [,]  Y. Arist. [,] Joseph, Marriam, &
Alexandra.


Welcome my dearest, sweetest, happiest,

All that my longings looke for; thus, and thus,

Like a rich chaine, my love shall hang about thee;                          195

And make the whole world doe thee reverence;

Nay weepe not Mother; come, I know your care,

And beare an equall burthen:  heere, O heere

Is the true tombe of Aristobulus.[29]

Q. Alex.

You can dissemble royally; but that                                          200

Cannot cure mine impostume.

Her.

                                Say not so;

You must forget the worke of accident.

[II.i. ]

Q. Alex.

    Of accident?  of plotted massacre;

    Murder beyond example:  but there's left

    A hell to reckon with.

Her.

                     Good sweet, no more;          205

    Let not your judgement wrong you to suspect

    Mine innocence unjustly; for, I vow,

    Never came death so neare me; or did force

    My teares in such aboundance; but you know,

    Earth must not question Heaven:  yet to shew       210

    My faire affection to your princely sonne;

    Within an urne of gold, Ile lodge his bones;

    And to his funerall rites, adde such a pompe,

    As shall amaze invention; and besides,

    There's not an eye in all Jerusalem,          215

    But shall drop sorrow for him.

Q. Alex.

                     Funerals are

    But wretched satisfactions.

Kip.

                     Note this pride.

Sal.

    Yes, and her daughters sullennesse.

Her.

    Why looks my lovely Marriam downward, & dejects

[II.i.]

The glory of her bright eye?  I had thought                    220

My safe returne (which strikes a generall joy

Through Juda and Jerusalem, and makes

Mount Sion so triumphant) had not had

The power to kill her comforts:  lovely one;

How have I lost thy friendship; or, what fiend            225

Sends this divorce betwixt us?

Mar.

Your owne dissimulation. Cruell Sir;

Y'ave dealt unjustly with me, and prophan'd

A temple held you sacred.

Her.

What, your selfe?

O doe not speake it; for to that blest shrine            230

I have beene so religious, that the world

Hath oft condemnd me of idolatry:

And can you then accuse me?

Mar.

Yes, and call

Your owne heart to be witnesse.

Her.

Let me then

Be strucke with fearefull thunder.

Mar.

Sir, take heed;            235

Vengeance is quicke in falling.

[II.i. ]

Her.

Let it come:

You call a love in question, that's as just

As equity or goodnesse; by that power--

Mar.

Come, you will now be perjur'd; but Ile stay

That imputation from you: what became         240

Of your affection, when you bound that man;

If you miscarried in your worke at Rome,

That he should see me poyson'd?[30]  Start you now?

O, twas a venom'd complot.

Her.

Sir, a word:

Y'are a faithlesse young man; and have lost        245

The great hope I had in you.

Ant.

By my life,

Hopes, and all fruitfull wishes; I'm of this

As innocent as Silence:  if my lips

Ere open'd to relate it; let me feele

Some sodaine fatall judgement:  Gracious Sir,     250

Search out this secret further, 'twill be found

There is more treason breeding.

Her.

I'm resolv'd.

Madam, you have accus'd me; and I stand

[II.i.]

    So strongly on mine owne truth, that you must

    Discover your informers:  by that love           255

    Once you did faine* to beare me; by that faith

    Which should linke married couples; by the awe,

    Duty and truth of women; or if these

    Be canceld with your fury; yet by that

    Great power your King hath ore you, and to shun    260

    The scourge of torments, which I sollemnly

    Will try to the extreamest; heere I bind,

    Nay, doe command you, that unfainedly

    You tell me who inform'd you.

Mar.

                  You have laid

    So great commandments on me, that I dare       265

    In no wise disobey you.  Sir, it was

    Lord Joseph that inform'd me.

Her.

                  Ha; Joseph!

    O my abused confidence!

Ant.

              Now it workes.

Kip.

    The fire begins to kindle.

Sal.

              But Ile bring

    Fuell that shall inflame it.           270

[II.i.]

Her.

    Joseph? was't Joseph? then tis time to feele

    My cold dull unbelieving.

Jos.

                  O pardon me;

    It was my love, not malice.

Her.

                No, your lust,

    And you shall buy it dearely: call a guard.       Enter Animis,

    Have I for this so often lost my selfe           and a guard.

    Within the labyrinth of her wanton eyes;           276

    And am I now repaid with treachery:

    Ceaze on those wretched creatures; Salumith,

    Stand forth, and what thy knowledge can approve

    Against those traytors, speake it; now mine eare     280

    Lies open to my safety.

Ant.

                Bravely speake,

    You shall have strong supporters; now his eare

    Is open, see you fill it.

Sal.

                Doubt me not.

    Great Sir, with confidence as full of truth,

    As they are full of treason; I averre,            285

    These, in your absence, have abus'd your bed,

    With most incestuous foule adultery.

[II.i.]

Mar.

    All that's like goodnesse shield me.

Jos.

    Woman, looke up;

    The vault of heaven is marble;* this untruth        290

    Will make it fall to kill thee.

Sal.

                             Let it come,

    If I speake ought unjustly; all my words,

    My blood and oath shall seale to.*


    Enter Antipater,* Pheroas, and Achitophel.


Antip.

    Good, let my love perswade thee; doe not buze

    Such foule things in his eares; his Majestie        295

    Is too much mov'd already.

Phe.

                        Good my Lord,

    Let me discharge my duty.

Ant.

                      Nay, for that,

    I dare not to withstand; yet, questionlesse,

    The Queene is not so wicked. --Goe, put home;

    Y'ave all things to assist you: --sirrah Jew,        300

    Forget not thy preferment.

[II.i.]

Ach.

                         Feare me not.

Her.

   How now, what tumult's that?

Phe.

   O my dread Lord,

   Grant me your gracious pardon; I must tell

   A sad and heavy story; yet most true:             305

   And yet 'gainst such a person, as I feare

   Your eare will not receive it.

Her.

                     Speake; 'gainst whom?

Phe.

   Against the Queene.

Mar.

   O sacred Truth, but thee,

   I have nor sword, nor armour.

Her.

                   Utter it.            310

Phe.

   Since your departure, to my hands she brought

   This fatall violl; saying, Pheroas,

   Thou art the Kings cup-bearer; by my love

   I charge thee, when his Majesty shall call

   For wine, give him this potion; tis a draught    315

   Shall crowne thee with great fortunes:  I desir'd

[II.i.]

To know the nature; shee, with solemne oathes,

Swore it was nothing but a wholsome drinke,

Compounded with such art; that, tasting it,

You would doate of her beauty, and become                    320

A very slave to her perfections:

I promis'd to performe it; yet my feare

Arguing with my judgement, made me try

The vertue on a spaniel; and I found

It was an odious poyson. 31

Omnes.

Wonderfull!                                                   325

Phe.

After this triall, I demanded then,

From whom her Highnesse had it:  she affirm'd,

From the Lord Joseph; but by stricter search,

I found this Jew was he compounded it.

Ach. 32

I doe confesse the Queene of Israel                          330

Commanded me to try my utmost skill

In this most strong confection; said it was

To prove the force of simples:  I, her slave,

Durst not to disobay her; yet suspect

Made me reveale it to this noble-man.                        335

Her.

How answer you this treason?

[II.i.]

Mar.

Silently.

Her.

Thats a confession.

Mar.

Why, as good be dumbe,

As speake to eares are glewd up; or a faith

Thats arm'd against beleeving:  but (great Sir)

If either of these open; then, beleev't,                          340

Was never wrong'd a greater innocence.

Jos.

Malice hath wrought upon us, and oretane

Our guiltlesse lives with vengeance:  hell it selfe

Is not more false then these are; yet, I know,

Nothing can save us but a miracle.                               345

Her.

The guilty ever plead thus; cursed chance,

To have my joyes devoure me:  but, tis done;

Princes, your eares and counsels.                    Herod whispers

Q. Alex.                                              with Ant. [,] the

Ha! is't so,                                         Princes and Pheroas.

Hath Mischiefe got the conquest; then tis time                   350

To change my disposition, and deceive

Those which would else deceive me; in this kinde,

It skils not whom we injure, whom we blinde.

[II.i. ]

P. Alex.

    Sir, of my life all this is counterfait,

    And this great divell inchants you; for these slaves,     355

    They speake but what is taught them.

Y. Arist.

    On my life,

    Our royall mother's guiltlesse; doe not let

    Their hatefull malice step betweene her life,

    And your most gracious favour.

Her.

                              Princely youths,     360

    Nature and love deceives you:  wretched things,

    What can you say to stay destruction?

Mar.

    That w'are the Kings, and none are innocent,

    Unlesse he please to thinke so.

Q. Alex.

                            Impudent!

    Is that all thou canst utter?  Have I liv'd     365

    To see thee grow thus odious, to forsake

    The chast imbracements of a royall bed,

    For an incestuous letcher; to become

    The peoples scorne, the honest matrons curse,

    The tribes disgrace, and Israels obloquy;     370

    Nay more, the whole worlds wonder, and a staine

[II.i.]

    Nere to be washt off from Jerusalem?

    O mine afflicted honor![33]

Kip.

                        Heere's a change.

Sal.

    A tempest never lookt for.

Q. Alex.

    Packe for shame,                        375

    Runne to thine owne destruction: what, a whore?

    A poysoning whore? a baudy murderesse?

    Nay, more; a treacherous strumpet? O that Heaven

    Had made mine anger lightning, that it might

    Destroy thee in a moment.

Mar.

                       Madam, stay;          380

    Can your true goodnesse thinke me culpable?

Q. Alex.

    Is it not prov'd apparant?

Mar.

    Then be dumbe,

    Be dumbe for ever Marriam; if you thinke

    I can be guilty, who is innocent?        385

    Madam, you are my mother; O call up

    Your worst imaginations, all the scapes

    Both of mine infance, childhood or ripe yeares,

    And if the smallest shadow in them all

[II.i. ]

Betoken such an error, curse me still,                                    390

Let me finde death with horror; otherwise,

Silence and patience helpe me.  Sir, tis fit

You plead your owne cause; I am conquered.

Jos.

There's but one true Judge over Israel,

And Hee knowes I am guiltlesse.

Her.

                                   Tis the plea                           395

Of every guilty person:  Animis,

Convay those wicked creatures,[34] with your guard,

Unto the market-place, and there in sight

Of all the people, cause the hangman take

Their curst head from their bodies.[35]                                  400

P. Alex.

Stay, great Sir,

Doe not an act t'amaze all Israel;

O looke with mercies eyes upon the Queene;

The innocent Queene our mother; let not slaves

Blast her with false reproches; be a god                                 405

And finde out truth by miracle.

Her.

                                   No more.

Y. Arist.

No more? yes sure, if every word I speake

Should naile me to destruction:  mighty Sir,

[II.i.]

    Favour your owne repentance, doe not spill

    The innocent bloud unjustly; for th'account         410

    Is heavy as damnation:  to your selfe,

    And to your owne, become a Daniel.

Her.

    Ile heare no more.

P. Alex.

    O sacred Sir, you must;

    Upon my knees I begge compassion;         415

    Compassion for my mother.

Y. Arist.

                  To this ground

    Weele grow eternally;* till you vouchsafe

    To grant her mercy; or to give her cause

    A larger course of tryall.

Her.

                  Once againe,

    I charge you to forget her.

P. Alex.

                  How, forget         420

    The chast wombe which did beare us; or the paps

    Which gave us sucke?*  Can there in Nature be

    A lethargie so frozen?

Y. Arist.

                Nay, what's more;

    Can we forget her holy stocke,[36] deriv'd

[II.i.]

　From all the blessed patriarchs, in whom　　　　　425

　You and our selves are glorious?  O, dread Sir,

　Have mercy on her goodnesse.

P. Alex.

　　　　　　　　　　Mercy, Sir.

Her.

　How am I vext with importunity;

　Away to execution:  if againe

　I doe command tis fatall.

Y. Arist.

　　　　　　　　　And if we　　　　　　430

　Indure it, let us perish; brother draw,　　The Princes draw.

　And let our good swords guard her:  Sir, y'ave broke

　A linke in Natures best chaine; and her death,

　Converts us to your mortall enemies.

Her.

　What; am I brav'd by traitors?  Villaines, force　　　435

　Way to the execution, or you perish.

P. Alex.

　Mother, hold life but one houre and wee'l rescue you.


　The Princes force through the guard; Antipater drawes & stands

　before Herod; all the rest convey away the prisoners;

　Alexandra wringing her hands.

[II.i. ]

[Her. ]

    Did ever kings owne bowels thus become

    The Typhon of sedition; or, can't be,

    I could beget these serpents?  Ift be so[, ]          440

    Under the Aetna of their damned pride,

    Ile smoother and consume them.

Ant.

                  Sir, I know

    Your wisedome such, as can discerne what tis

    At once to feare, to suffer, and to dye,

    By th'hand of sterne ambition; which, ith'end,      445

    Makes still her habitation like the place

    Where poyson growes, so naked and so bare

    That dust disdaines t'abide there.

Her.

                  Passing true;

    But Ile root out that vengeance:  yet againe,

    When I awake my memory, to looke          450

    Upon her sweetnesse, goodnesse, and conceive,

    That no affaire, no wisedome, or fond zeale,

    Which oft attainteth others, could touch her;

    O then, me thinkes, I might at least have breath'd,

    Before I had condemn'd her; Justice should      455

    Ith darke of these confusions, borne a torch

    Before Truth and mine anger:  but alas,

    Folly and rashnesse led me; and I've lost

[II.i. ]

    All my delight at one throw.  Antipater,

    Goe, runne, flye; O, stay the execution.[37]          460

Ant.

    Willingly.  Yet please you first to thinke

    Whether the act hurt not your Majestie;

    Kings, in these waighty causes, must not play

    At fast and loose; their wordes are oracles;

    And judgement should pursue them.          465

Her.

    Good, no more; goe stay the execution.

Ant.

    Not on earth is there a man more willing;

    Yet, when kings condemne themselves of rashnesse,

    Who can blame contempt to follow after?

Her.

    Lord to see how time is lost with talking.          470

Antip.

    I am gone.                    Offers to goe and returnes.

    Yet Sir, beleev't; the Majesty which strikes

    Against comtempt shall nere recover it.

Her.

    Yet againe.

Ant.

    Sir, I can vanish quickly; yet, behold,          475

    Heere's one can save my labour.          Enter Pheroas.

---

475.  Ant.) Quarto: Ant,

[II.i.]

Her.

    Speake my Lord; where is my Queene?

    O, where's my Marriam?

Phe.

                Sir, she is dead.

Her.

    Dead?  Be the world dead with her; for on earth

    There's no life but her glory:  yet declare            480

    How dyed the wofull lady?

Phe.

               Like a saint.

    Like did I say? O Sir, so farre beyond,

    That never saint came neere her president:

    She did not goe, as one that had beene led

    To take a violent parting; but as Fate            485

    Had in her owne hands thrust her destiny,

    Saying, or live or dye:  whilst she, that knew

    The one and th'others goodnesse, did agree

    Onely to dye as th'act most excellent.

    Her mothers bitter railings, all the cries          490

    Of the amazed people, mov'd not her;

    No not one poore small twinckle of her eye:

    But, with a constancie, that would outface

    The brazen front of terror; she assends

[II.i.]

Up to the fatall scaffold; and but once                              495

Lookt round about the people:  then lifts up

Her snow-white hands to heaven;

Talkes to it as if she had beene in it:  then fals downe

Upon her humble knees; which, as they bent,

You might behold humility retire                                     500

Downe to her heart; and left within her eyes

Nothing but sweetnesse flaming:  whilst upon

And round about her, majestie did hang,

And cloath her as a garment:  to be briefe,

Shee tooke the stroke, not as a punishment;                         505

But a reward; so saint-like hence she went.

Her.

Enough, too much; th'ast slaine me Pheroas;

O, I have lost in her death more true joyes,

Then Heaven can give or, earth is worthy of:

I am a traitor to my selfe and love;                                510

To Nature, vertue, beauty, excellence;

I have destroy'd the whole world; for but her,

It had no soule, nor moving; no delight,

No triumph, glory, or continuance:

I cannot live to lose her; call her backe,                          515

Or I shall dye complaining.[38]

Ant.

This is strange [:]

Can the dead be awaken'd?

[II.i.]

Her.

Easily Sir,

My sighes shall breath life in her; and my voyce

Rouze her, as doth a trumpet; nay, more loud

Than either winde or thunder:  canst thou thinke          520

That I can live without her; she, to whom

The whole world was a theater, where men

Sate viewing her good actions; she, that had

As much right unto Paradise, as kings

Have to their courts and kingdomes; shee that lent          525

Mintage to other beauties; for, none are

Or good, or faire, but such as lookt like her:

Shee, in whose body sweetly was contain'd

Th'Easterne spicery, the Westerne treasure,

And all the world holds happy:  may it be          530

That I can live and want her? or, could I

With one sad breath destroy her? she, that had

(In her owne thoughts) read all that ere was writ,

To better, or instruct us:  shee, that knew

Heaven so well on earth; that, being there,          535

Shee finds no more then she did thinke on heere;

And have I kild her?  She, whose very dreames

Were more devout then our petitions;

Have I prophan'd that temple?  Fall, O fall

---

519.  loud) Quarto:  lou'd

[II.i.]

Downe to the ground and perish; nere looke up,                540

But when or blastings, mildewes, lightenings,

Or poysonous serenes strike thee.  Herod, heere,

O heere, digge up thy grave with sorrow.

Ant.

Fie, tis unfit Greatnesse should yeeld to passion.

Her.

Y'are a foole;                                                 545

He that not mournes for her, will never mourne;

But is worse then the Divell.  Marriam;

O Marriam; thou that through the spheares

(As through so many golden beads) hast runne,

In one poore moment, to felicity;                              550

Looke downe upon thy vassall, me thy slave,

And see how much I languish:  let thine eye

Guild my complaints, and cheere my misery.

Phe.

O royall Sir, take better comfort;

There was nere on earth a creature worth your sorrow.          555

Her.

Sir, you lie; deadly and falsly; for she doth deserve

The teares of men and angels:  shee, O shee,

Of whom the ancients prophesied, when first

They made all vertues females; she, that was

The first and best faire copie, from whose lines             560

The world might draw perfection:  she, not worth

[II.i.]

    The teares of all thats living?  Dulnesse, goe;

    Packe from my sight for ever:  O, 'twas thou,

    Thou that didst make me kill her:  hence, avaunt;

    By all that's good or holy; if, from hence           565

    Thou ere presume to see me, or come neere

    The place of my abiding; 'tis thy death,*

    As certaine as Fate spoke it.[39]

Phe.

    O my Lord.

Her.

    Away; reply, and I will kill thee.              570

Ant.

    Do not offend him further; vanish Sir.        Exit Pheroas.


Enter Animis.


Ani.

    To armes my Lord, to armes:  your princely sonnes,

    Attended by the people, stand betweene

    The towne of Bethlem and Jerusalem;

    Their ensignes spread, their bowes bent, and their swords

    Waving like wings of eagles:  Sir, they vow       576

    Revenge for their mothers death.

Her.

    On whom?

[II.i. ]

[Ani. ]

    On you, the citty; but especially,

    Upon the Prince Antipater.

Her.

                       No more,             580

    Th'are angry surges, which with one poore blast,

    Ile make fall to the center;* troubled thoughts,

    Rest till this storme be over:  happy man,

    Ile make thee tread upon them; this day shall

    Be thy coronation; but their funerall.      Exe. all but Ant.

Ant.

    Twas a brave lesson that Egystus taught,      586

    And Clitemnestra writ religiously:

    Sinne safest way to sinne; none or alone; both excellent.

    Yet Herod lives unwrong'd and unremov'd.

    The sonnes of Oedipus, in life, nor after death,    590

    Agreed but once; which was, t'imprison Oedipus;*

    An act of no small wonder: O, but boyes,

    Ile mount a world above you; t'imprison, is

    Still to have danger neere me:  tut, tis death,

    Death that my aymes doe shoote at:  Ile invent    595

    What none shall alter:  fie, tis nothing worth,

    By worth, by birth, by choyce,* by chance to bee a king;

    But so to climbe I choose, as all may feare and wonder;

    Feare to attempt the like, and wonder how I wrought it;

    Curst be he (in this case) that craves his fathers blessing;

[II.i. ]

My throane must be my fathers monument;                    601

My raigne built on his ruine:  but how? how? witlesse, how?

Aske how, and seeke a crowne?  By poyson; no, by sword;

Sword; no, by subtilty:  O hell awake, awake;

And once for all instruct me.                              605


Dumbe shew.

Musique:  and, enter Miscipsa, Jugurth, Adherball, Hiempsall,

Miscipsa makes them joyne hands, and gives each a crowne, and

departs:  then in mounting the tribunall, Hiempsall and Adher-

ball sit close to keepe out Jugurth, he divides them by force,

Hiempsall offers to draw, and Jugurth stabs him; Adherball

flies and comes in againe with the Roman senators, they seeme

to reconcile them; and being departed, Jugurth stabs Adherball,

and leaves at Antipaters feete a scrowle.*


O resolute Jugurth; what afford'st thou me?

Non mordent mortui; dead men doe not bite:

True, noble bastard:  Jugurth, in thy light

Thy brothers dwelt; O  Jugurth, so doe mine:

Thou kild'st them Jugurth; Jugurth, so must I.           610

Thus sing we severall descant* on one plain-song, kill:

Foure parts in one, the meane excluded quite:

The base sings deepely, kill; the counter-tenor, kill;

The tenor, kill, kill; the treble, kill, kill, kill:

In diapason kill is the unison, seaven times redoubled;   615

[II.i.]

And so oft must I kill:  as, first the King,

(His wife is past) two sonnes, two brethen,* and a sister;

And thinke not but I can:  can; nay, but I will:

I am no puny* in these documents:

The tyger, tasting blood; finds it to[o] sweet to leave it:     620

The hauke, once made to prey, takes all delight in preying;

The virgin, once deflour'd, thinks pleasure to grow cõmon;*

And can I then stop in a middle way?*

Cloze fountaines, rivers dry; pluck up the roots bowes perish;

Banish the sunne, the moone and starres doe vanish:            625

And, were it to obscure the world, and spoyle

Both man and beast, Nature, and every thing;

Yet would I doo't; and why?  I must, and will be King.

Kingly Antipater.                                        Exit.


[Enter Josephus as Antipater leaves.]


Josephus.

Never grew pride more high, more desperate;              630

Nor ever could the arrogance of man

Finde out a breast more large and spacious:

But Fate and he must wrestle.  Let mee now

Intreat your worthy patience, to containe

Much in imagination; and, what words                    635

Cannot have time to utter; let your eyes

Out of this dumbe shew, tell your memories.

[II.i.]

Dumbe shew.

Enter at one dore, with drums and colours, P. Alexander, and

Y. Aristobulus, with their army; at another, Herod and An-

tipater, with their army:  as they are ready to encounter, enter

Augustus with his Romans betweene them; they all cast downe

their weapons at his feet and kneels; he raises Herod and sets

him in his chayre, makes Alexander and Aristobulus kisse his

feet; which done, they offer to assaile Antipater, Herod steps

between, Augustus reconciles them; then whispering with Herod,

Augustus takes three garlands and crownes the three sonnes,

Herod placing Antipater in the midst, and so all depart,

Antipater using ambitious countenances.[40]


Josephus.

The sonnes of Marriam, having met the King,

Are ready for encounter; but are staid

By th'awe of great Augustus, at whose feete                640

They cast their lives and weapons:  hee, with frownes

Chides the two angry Princes; yet commands

The father to forgive them; peace is made:

Onely against Antipater they bend

The fury of their courage; which the King                645

Withstands and reconciles them:  all made sound;

Augustus gives them garlands, and installs

Them equall captaines over Palestine:

But yet Antipater, by Herods meanes,

[II.i. & III.i.]

Gets the precedence and priority:                              650

How in that throng he justles; tis your eyes,

And not my tongue must censure:  thus we hope

Our scale is still assending; and you'le finde

Better, and better; and the best behinde.*                    Exit.


Finis actus secundae[.]

---

Act. 3. Scoena 1.


Enter Salumith, and Lyme the mason.


Sal.

You must take my directions.

Lym.

Any thing your Ladiship will have me.

Sal.

Thou shalt informe his Majesty; his sons hired thee,

when his Highnes should approach to view the buildings,

by seeming chance to throw some stone upon him, which        5

might crush him to pieces.  Do this and thou shalt gaine by't.[41]

---

652.  thus) Quarto: this        S.D.  Scoena) Quarto:  Scoena.

[III.i. ]

Lym.

A halter, or some worse thing; for (Madam) the least

stone that is imployd about the Temple, is 20. cubits broad,

and 8. thicke,[42] and thats able to break a mans necke without

a halter.                                                           10

Sal.

No matter.

Lym.

Nay, and it be no matter for breaking a neck (though it be

an ill joynt to set) Ile venter a swearing for't.

Sal.

Doe, and live rich and happy; hold, there's gold.

Lym.

Nay, if I can get my living by swearing and forswearing;      15

Ile never use other occupation.                    Enter Handsaw.

Han.

Neighbour Lyme; newes, newes, newes.

Lym.

What newes, neighbour Handsaw?

Han.

Marry Sir, Charity has got a new coate; for I saw a

beadle just now whipping on statute-lace.*                      20

Sal.

And what's become of Liberality?

[III.i.]

Han.

    Cry you mercy Lady, faith she went like a baud at a carts

    taile, roaring up and downe; but her purse was empty.

Sal.

    Th'art deceiv'd [;] her hand is ever open,

    And to desert shees free; behold else.       [Gives them money.]

Han.

    This is more of Liberality, (as you call it) then I      26

    have found, since I began first to build the Temple.

Lym.

    Or I either.

Sal.

    You shall have more,

    Ile poure it on in showers; performe but my commandments.    30

Han.

    Madam, by my handsaw & compasse, I will do any thing; say,

    speake, sweare, and forsweare any thing your Ladiship can

    invent or purchase.

Sal.

    Hark your eares.                  Whisper.

Han.

    Hum, ha; pretty, pretty; Ile play my part to a tittle;    35

    neighbour, looke to yours: nay, and Ile doe it presently;

    for the King is now comming to the Temple, and I came to

    call you neighbour; wee'l doe it there.

[III.i. ]

Lym.

What else; a man may bee forsworne in any place,

citty, court or country, has no difference.                    40

Sal.

About it then; be constant wary and y'are fortunate.

Lym.

Feare us not, if you want any more to be forsworne,

give me your money, Ile presse a dozen tradesmen shall doe

it as well as any Scribe in all Jerusalem.

Han.

I or Publican either.

Sal.

                Away then.                    Exe. Lym. & Han.

Thus catch we hearts with gold; thus spiders can              46

Poyson poore flyes, and kill the innocent man.


Enter Antipater with a letter, and Animis.


Ant.

Be swift as lightning; for the cause requires it:

Such paper-plots are invisible goblins;

Pinching them most, which doe least injury.                   50

Y'are arm'd with full instructions.

-----------

48.   Ant.) Quarto:  Ani.

[III.i.]

Ani.

                                Sir, I am.

Ant.

    Your letters are Chrysanders, and not mine.[43]

Ani.

    I know it well.

Ant.

    Away then, outflye eagles; yet Sir, harke;

    Carry your countnance wisely, seeme to be          55

    A saint in thy delivery.

Ani.

                          Sir, your care

    Makes you too curious, feare me not.         Exit Animis.

Ant.

    Within there.                          Enter Hillus.

Hil.

    Did your Excellence call?

Ant.

    I did; what, is your lesson got?             60

Hil.

    My Lord, unto a sillable; my tongue

    Hath poyson for your purpose, and I am

    Confirm'd in every circumstance.

Ant.

    The time, (at night;) the place, (the bed-chamber;)

    The manner, (arm'd;) the instruments, (their swords.)[44]    65

[III.i.]

Hil.

    Tut, this is needlesse; Sir, my quality

    Needs not a twice instruction.

Ant.

    Nobly said; hold, there's gold.

Hil.

    This is a good perswader; right or wrong,

    Treasure will make the dumbe man use his tongue.*        70

Ant.

    True; tis the sicke mans balme, the usurers pledge,

    And indeed all mens maisters; goe away,        Exit Hillus.

    The time's ripe for thy purpose; thus these slaves

    Runne post to hell for shadowes;* ha, Salumith:

    O my best aunt and mistris; y'are well met:        75

    Never were times so tickle;* nor, I thinke,

    Stood innocence in more danger: would my life

    Were lost, to thrust feares from you.

Sal.

    Why, princely Nephew, I've no cause to feare.

Ant.

    Tis well you are so arm'd; indeed, a life        80

    So good as yours, free,* and religious,

    Thinkes not on feare, or ill mens actions:

    Yet Madam, still your state is slippery;

    Believe it while these Princes doe survive,

[III.i.]

    And dreame how you accus'd the Mother-Queene,         85

    They still will practise 'gainst you.[45]

Sal.

                                    Yes, and you;

    The High-Priests death, and Marriams tragedy,

    Will be objected 'gainst you.

Ant.

                            Tis confest;

    W'are both marks of their vengeance.

Sal.

                           Yet so farre

    Beyond them, Ile not feare them; heere's my hand,       90

    I've markt them for destruction:  since our fates

    Have equall danger; tis no reason but

    They doe injoy like triumph; once againe,

    Believe it, they are sinking.

Ant.

                      Nobly said,

    Mirror of women, angell, goddesse, saint.          95


    Enter Tryphon the barber, with a case of instruments.


Sal.

    Peace, no more; heere comes mine instrument.

Ant.

    What, this; the Kings barber, your doting Amorite?*[46]

[III.i.]

Sal.

    The same, observe him.

Try.

    O blessed combe; thou spotlesse ivory,

    With which my mistris Salumith once daind        100

    To combe the curious felters* of her hayre,

    And lay each threed in comely equipage;*

    Sleepe heere in peace for ever; let no hand

    (But mine henceforth) be ever so adacious,

    Or daring as to touch thee.        105

Ant.

    Pittiful foole, goe sleepe, or thoult runne mad els.

Try.

    Sizers, sweet sizers; sharpe, but gentle ones;

    That once did cut the locks of Salumith;

    Making them in humility hang downe

    On either side her cheekes, as 'twere to guard        110

    The roses, that there flourish:  O, goe rest,

    Rest in this peacefull case; and let no hand

    Of mortall race prophane you.

Ant.

                      Sfoote, the slave

    Will begger himselfe with buying new instruments.

Sal.

    O tis a piece of strange idolatry.        115

[III.i.]

Try.

Tooth-pick, deare tooth-pick; eare-pick, both of you

Have beene her sweet companions; with the one

I've seene her picke her white teeth; with the other

Wriggle so finely worme-like in her eare;

That I have wisht, with envy, (pardon me)                    120

I had beene made of your condition:

But tis too great a blessing.

Ant.

What, to be made a tooth-picke?

Sal.

Nay, youle spoyle all, if you interrupt him.

Try.

Salumith, O Salumith;                                        125

When first I saw thy golden lockes to shine,

I brake my glasse; needing no face, but thine:

When at those corrall lips, I was a gazer;

Greedy of one sweet touch, I broke my razor:

When to thy cheekes, thou didst my poore eyes call;         130

Away flew sizers, bason, balls* and all:

Only the crisping-irons I kept most deare;

To doe thee service heere and every where.

Sal.

Not every where good Triphon, some place still

Must be reserv'd for other purposes.                        135

[III.i.]

Try.

    Bright go-o-o-desse.

Sal.

                 Well proceede;

    What, at a stand? has true love got the power,

    To strike dumbe such a nimble wit?

Ant.

    Cry hem,* pluck up thy heart man? what, a polling

    shaving squire, and strucke dead with a woman?          140

Sal.

    Nothing so, he does but mocke, he loves not Salumith.

Try.

    Not love you Lady? O strange blasphemy!

Ant.

    Faith, what wouldst thou do now but for a kisse of her hand.

Try.

    What would I do? what not? O any thing.

    Ile number all those hayres my sizers cut,             145

    And dedicate those numbers* to her shrine;

    A breath more loathsome then the stench of Nile,

    Ile rectifie, and, for her sake, make pleasant;

    A face more black then any Aethiope,

    Ile scoure as white as silver; to attaine            150

    But one touch of her finger, I'de beget

    Things beyond wonder; stab, poyson, kill,

    Breake mine owne necke, my friends, or any mans.

[III.i.]

Sal.

    Spoke like a daring servant; harke thine eare;

    Doe this and have thy wishes.          *They whisper.*

Try.

    What, but this?                          156

Ant.

    No more beleeve it; why, tis nothing man;

    Only, it asks some seriousnes and art,

    By which to move the King, and gaine beleefe.

Try.

    But shall I have a kisse from that white hand,     160

    Which gripes my heart within it?

Sal.

    Sir, you shall; tis there, pay your devotion.

Try.

    Then by this kisse Ile do it; honey kisse    *Kisses her hand.*

    There's resolution in thee, and I'm fixt

    To doe it swiftly, quickly; from my lip          165

    Thy sweet taste shall not part, till I have spoke

    All that your wishes looke for:  boast of this;

    Y'ave bought two princes lives with one poore kisse.    *Exit.*

Ant.

    Spoke like a noble servant.

Sal.

                   Nephew, true;

    Let him and's follies wrestle; from their birth    170

[III.i.]

We will bring out our safeties; villaines, we know

Are sometimes stilts, on which great men must goe.


Enter Herod with his sword drawne, in his other hand a letter,

driving before him P. Alexander, and Y. Aristobulus, Animis,

Hillus, Lime and Handsaw following Herod; Antip. steps betweene

Herod and the Princes.


P. Alex. [,] Y. Arist.

Sir, as y'are royall, heare us.

Her.

Villaines, traytors, vipers.

Ant.

In the name

Of goodnesse and of good men; what hand dare                    175

Be rais'd against his soveraigne? Gracious Sir,

Let not your rage abuse you; there's none heere

That your word cannot slaughter.

Her.

Give me way;

Shall my owne blood destroy me? that I gave

Ile sacrifice to justice.

P. Alex.

Yet Sir, hold.                    180

Heare but our innocent answere.

[III.i.]

Y. Arist.

                             If we prove

   Guilty, let tortures ceaze us.

Sal.

                          O my Lord,

   Tis a becomming justice; heare them speake.

Her.

   What, villaines that are arm'd against me?

Sal.

   Tis not so; Nephewes, deare Nephewes,               185

   Throw at his Highnes feete, these ill becomming weapons;

   In this case, they doe not guard but hurt you.

P. Alex.

   We obey; and, with our weapons offer up our lives,

   To have our cause but heard indifferently.

Y. Arist.

   Sir, there's no greater innocence on earth           190

   Injur'd then our alleageance:  let but truth

   Accuse us in a shadow; spare us not.

Her.

   But truth accuse you?  O strange impudence!

   Th'art not of brasse, but adamant:  seest thou this,

   This man you hir'd with stone to murder me;       195

   This man with timber; both you wrought to staine

   The sacred building with foule paricide.  Is not this true?

[III.i.]

Lym. [, ] Han.

   Most true (my Lord) wee will both bee forsworne* unto it.

P. Alex.

   Falshood, th'art grown a mighty one, when these;

   These slaves shall murder princes.

Her.

                      No, not these [; ]       200

   Your vilde acts doe destroy you:  speake, my Lord;

   Did not you see these in the dead of night,

   Arm'd with their weapons, watch at my chamber doore,

   Intending to assault me?

Hil.

              Tis most true;

   And had I not with threats and some exclaimes      205

   Remov'd them, you had perisht.

Ant.

             Wonderfull.

P. Alex.

   O Truth, for shame awaken; this slave will

   Exile thee from all mankinde.

Her.

            What, doth this

   Bristle your guilty spirits?  No, Ile come

   Neerer unto your treasons; heer's your hands,      210

   Your own hands, most unnaturall:  Sister, see;

   See, mine Antipater; (for I know, you both

[III.i.]

Are perfect in their hands and characters)

This letter did they traitrously convey

Unto Chrysander, which commands our powers,                      215

And conquests won in Greece; inciting him

To breake his firme alleageance, and to joyne

His strength with theirs, to worke our overthrow.

Speake, our Centurion; did not you receive

This letter from Chrysander?                                     220

Ani.

My Lord, I did.

Her.

And that it is their owne hands, witnesse you;

And you; and all that know them.

Sal.

I am strooke dumbe with wonder; I should sweare

This were your own hands Nephews.

Ant.

                            By my hopes;                     225

If it be false, tis strangely counterfeit;

The slave that did it had a cunning hand,

And neere acquaintance with you:  but, deare Sir,

It shall be gracious in you to conceive

The best of these misfortunes:  who, that knowes            230

The world, knowes not her mischieves; and how slaves

Are ever casting mines up;* for my part,

[III.i.]

    (Though there's no likelihood) I will suppose,

    This is, and may be counterfeit.

Sal.

                   And so will I.

Her.

    But never I, it is impossible.             235

P. Alex.

    Sir, I beseech you, howsoere you lose

    The force of Nature, or the touch of blood;

    Lose not the use of justice; that should live,

    When both the rest are rotten:  all these proofes

    Are false as slander, and the worke hew'd out     240

    Only by malice; when w'are tane away,

    Tis you your selfe next followes:  why alasse,

    We are your armour; he that would strike home,

    And hit you soundly, must unbuckle us.

Y. Arist.

    Besides Sir, please you either send, or call     245

    Chrysander home (whom we have ever held,

    A noble, free, and worthy gentleman)

    And, if he doe accuse us; we will throw

    Our lives to death with willingnesse; nay more,

    Plead guilty to their slanders.

Ant.

                  In my thoughts     250

    This is a noble motion; heare them Sir.

[III.i.]

Sal.

　　It will renowne\* your patience; sacred Sir,

　　Let me begge for my nephewes; you have said

　　You tooke delight to heare me; heare me now.

Ant.

　　'Sfoote, y'are too earnest, and will spoyle us all;　　　　255

　　Begge with a scurvy cold parenthesis.

　　Sir, (though I know, in this case, minutes are

　　Irrecoverable losses) yet, you may

　　(If't please you) grant them their petition.[47]

Her.

　　I'm resolv'd,　　　　　　　　　　　　Enter Tryphon.

　　Chrysander shall be sent for: ha, how now?　　　　261

　　Why star'st thou? why art breathlesse?

Try.

　　　　　　　　　　　　　　O my Lord,

　　My gracious Lord, heare me; I must disclose

　　A treason foule and odious: these your sonnes,

　　Your princely sonnes, chiefly Prince Alexander,　　　　265

　　By fearefull threats, and golden promises,

　　Have labour'd me, that when I should be cald,

　　To trim your Highnesse beard, or cut your hayre;

　　I then should lay my razor to your throat,

　　And send you hence to heaven.[48]

---

255.　'Sfoote) Quarto: S'foote

[III.i.]

Ant. [,] Sal.

                               O unnaturall!          270

Her.

    Villaine, speake this againe.

P. Alex. [,] Y. Arist.

    Villaine, speake truth, feare Judgement.

Try.

    Briefly Sir, Prince Alexander, and Aristobulus

    Offer'd me heapes of gold to cut your throat,

    When I should trim or shave you.

Her.

                       From which, thus       275

    Mine owne hand shall secure me; villaine, die,     Stabs Tryph.

    That knew'st a way to kill me; and henceforth,

    What slave so ever dare to fill mine eare

    With tales of this foule nature, thus shall perish;[49]

    Ile not be tortur'd living:  where's my guard?        280

    Handle those treacherous young men; and, with cordes,

    Strangle them both immediately.

P. Alex.

                     Sir, O Sir.

Y. Arist.

    Heare us; but heare us.

Her.

              Never, I am deafe;

    Villaines, that hatch such execrable thoughts,

[III.i.]

    Unfit for noble spirits, shall not breath:          285

    Dispatch I say; for unto time Ile raise

    Such trophees of severity; that he

    Which reads your story with a bloody thought,

    Shall tremble and forsake it.*

P. Alex.

                     Yet that man

    Seeing your rigor, and our innocence,          290

    Shall turne his feare to pitty, and condemne

    The malice of your rashnesse: Sir, to dye

    Thus, as we doe, not guilty, is a death,

    Of all, most blest, most glorious; for, it is

    To brave death, not to feele it; and this end     295

    Revives us, but not kils us.

Y. Arist.

                  Brother, true;

    Let me imbrace thy goodnesse; for I know,

    The last gaspe of a death thus innocent,

    Hath no paine in it; and w'are sure to finde

    Sweetnesse ith' shortnesse, all content of minde.     300

Her.

    Pull, and dispatch them.[50]              They strangle

Ant.                              the Princes.

    This was well contriv'd.

Sal.

    An act worth imitation.

[III.i.]

Ant.

O, mighty Sir,

You have done justice bravely, on your head

Depends so many heads, and on your life                              305

The lives of such aboundance; that, beleev't,

Acts and consents must not alone be fear'd;

But words and thoughts; nay very visions,

In this case must be punish't:  ancient times,

(For princes safeties) made our dreames our crimes.          310

Her.

Tis true; and I am resolute to run a course,

T'affright the proud'st attempter; goe, convay

Those bodies unto buriall:  Antipater,

Come neere me man; th'art now the only branch

Left of this aged body; which, howere                                    315

Disdaind, for want of grafting;* yet, Ile now

Make thee the chiefe, the best, and principall.

It is our pleasure, that with winged speed,

Forthwith you passe to Rome; and, in our name,

Salute the great Augustus; say, that age, griefe,              320

And some naturall sicknesse, having made

My minde unfit for government; I crave,

He would confirme thee in the royalty:[51]

Which granted, I will instantly give up

To thee and to thy goodnesse, all I hold;                            325

Either in crowne, or greatnesse.

[III.i.]

Ant.

        Gracious Sir.

Her.

 Doe not crosse my commandment; for I know

 Thy sweet and modest temper:  but away;

 Fly in thy happy journey; I presage,

 Those which did hate my youth, will love mine age.   Exit.

Sal.

 Heeres a brave change, sweet Nephew; can you flye   331

 Above the pitch you play in?

Ant.

        No, sweet Aunt;

 Nor in my flight will leave you, could I shoote

 Through heaven, as through the ayre; yet would I beare

 Thy goodnesse ever with me:  how ere I rise,   335

 Tis you alone shall rule Jerusalem.

Sal.

 No, tis Antipater; goe, be fortunate:

 I've other plots in working.

Ant.

       So have I:

 The Kings death and her owne; till that be done,

 Nothing is perfect; th'halfe way is but runne.   340

 Ha! who's this?  the noble Pheroas?   Enter Pheroas sickly.

 What chance makes my deare uncle droope thus?

 Doe not give way to your discontentment.

[III.i.]

Phe.

    Pardon me, it is become my maister; spacious mindes

    Are not like little bosomes; they may presse           345

    And crush disgraces inward; but the great,

    Gives them full field to fight in; and each stroke

    Contempt doth strike is mortall.

Sal.

                Say not so;

    You may finde reparation.

Phe.

            Tell me where;

    Not upon earth; when Reputation's gone,          350

    Tis not in kings to bring her backe againe:

    I am a banisht out-cast, and what's more,

    The scorne of those gaze on me:  but a day

    Will come, of Visitation, when the King

    May wish these foule deeds undone.

Ant.

               Come, no more [;]     355

    W'are partners in your sorrowes; and how ere

    The King doth yet smile on us, we know well

    The word of any peasant hath full power

    To turne us topsie turvy.

Phe.

           Are you there?

    Nay, then you have got feeling.

[III.i.]

Sal.

                                Sensibly,               360

And feare, and will prevent it.


Enter Achitiphel singing, and Disease.


Ach.

Come buy you lusty gallants

    These simples which I sell;

In all our dayes were never seene like these,

    For beauty, strength, and smell:               365

Here's the king-cup, the paunce,* with the violet,

        The rose that loves the shower,

        The wholsome gilliflower,

        Both the cowslip, lilly,

        And the daffadilly;                 370

With a thousand in my power.          [Stops singing.]

Why where are all my customers?  none come buy

Of the rare Jew that sels eternity?

Dis.

Indeed Maister I'm of your minde; for none of your

drugges but sends a man to life everlasting.         375

Ach.

Peace knave I say, here's in this little thing

A jewell prizelesse, worthy of a king:

[III.i.]

    If any man so bold dare bee,

    Unseene, unknowne to coape with me,

    And give the price which I demand;[52]          380

    Heere's treasure worth a monarchs land.

Ant.

    Harke how the mountebanke sets out his ware.

Phe.

    O, tis a noble braggard; two dry'd frogs,

    An ownce of rats-bane, grease and staves-aker,

    Are all his ingredients.

Ant.

                       Peace for shame,        385

    Have charity before you; harke, observe.      Achit. sings.

Ach.

    Here's golden amaranthus,

        That true love can provoke;

    Of horehound store, and poysoning elebore,

        With the polipode of the oake:*        390

    Here's chast vervine* and lustfull eringo,*

        Health-preserving sage,

        And rue, which cures old age;

        With a world of others,

        Making fruitfull mothers:        395

    All these attend mee as my page.      [Stops singing.]

    Come buy, come buy, unknowne, unseene,

    The best that is, or ere hath beene:

    He that, not asking what, dare coape,

[III.i.]

    May buy a wealth past thought, past hope.          400

    Come buy, come buy, &c.

Dis.

    Maister, faith give mee leave to make my proclamation

    too, though not in rime; yet in as unsensible meeter

    as may be.

    If the Divell any man provoke,          405

    To buy's owne mischiefe in a poake;

    Or else, that hood-winckt he would climbe

    Up to the gallowes ere his time;

    If fooles would learne how to convay

    Their friends the quite contrary way;          410

    Come to my maister, they shall have

    Their wish; for hee's a crafty knave.

Ach.

    Sirrah, y'are saucy.

Dis.

    Fitter for your dish of knavery.

Ant.

    How now Achitophel; what's this curious drugge          415

    You make such boast of; may not I question it?

Ach.

    By no meanes Sir; he that will purchase this,

    Must pitch and pay; but aske no questions.

Ant.

    Not any?

[III.i.]

Ach.

      No, not any; doe you thinke

  Perfection needs encomiums?                        420

Dis.

  O my Lord, you may take my maisters word at all

  times; for, being a phisitian, hee's the onely best member

  in a common-wealth.

Sal.

  How prove you physitians the best members?

Dis.

  Because Madam, without them the world would increase     425

  so fast, that one man could not live by another.

Ant.

  Go to, y'are a mad knave:  but come Achitophel,

  How prize you this rich jewell?  If't be fit

  Only for kings; tis for Antipater.

Ach.

  The price is, two thousand drachmas.              430

Ant.

  Once Ile prove mad for my private pleasure,

  There's your price; give me the juell;

  Now it's bought & sold, you may disclose the full perfection.

Ach.

  There's reason for't my Lord, then know y'ave here

---

430.  drachmas) Quarto:  drachma's

[III.i.]

    The strongest quickest killingst poyson, which       435

    Learning or art ere utter'd; for one drop

    Kils sooner then a canon; yet so safe

    And free from all suspition, that no eye

    Shall see or swelling, pustule, or disease,

    Rage or affrighting torment:  but as death were     440

    Kissing and not killing, hence they goe

    Wrapt up in happy slumbers.

Ant.

    Tis enough;

    Goe, and as art produces things like these,

    Let me heare from you.         445

Ach.

    The Jew is all your creature.        Exit Achit.

Dis.

    Though (my Lord) I did not trouble my braines, yet I

    bestir'd my stumps ere this worke was brought to passe;

    I know the waight of the pestle and morter, and though

    my hands lost some leather; yet they found labour worthy

    your Lordships remembrance.        451

Ant.

    O, I understand you, goe, there's gold.      Exit Dis.

    Now my best Aunt and Uncle, see you this;

    Heeres but a little substance; yet a strength

    Able to beare a kingdome every way:      455

    This shall bring safety to us, and conduct

[III.i. & IV.i.]

    Herod the way to heaven: Uncle you

    Shall take it to your keeping; and as I

    Direct you by my letters, so imploy it;

    How ere stormes yet hang ore us, you shall finde,        460

    I have a deity can calme the winde.

Sal.

    Th'art excellent in all things; keepe thy way:

    What we admire, that we must obay.        Exeunt.


        Finis actus tertiae.


---


        Act. 4. Scoena 1.


Enter Alexandra, and her euenuch.


Q. Alex.

    But is it certaine Pheroas is so sicke,

    As Rumor doth give out?

Eue.

        Madam, he is ;

    Nor hath he ever since his banishment

    Cast up his heavy count'nance.

---

S. D. Scoena) Quarto: Scoena.

[IV.i.]

Q. Alex.

                                 Tis most strange;

But judgement still pursues him; yet Ile call          5

And visit his affliction; for although

His words accus'd my Marriam; tis his sinne

Not person, that I envy.

Eue.

                    Madam, here comes his lady.

Q. Alex.

O, you are wel encounter'd; I am sad         Ent. Adda.

That sadnesse thus afflicts you.              10

Ad.

I'm bound unto your goodnesse.

Q. Alex.

How fares your noble husband?

Ad.

Desperately ill;

His sicknesse Madam rageth like a plague,

Once spotted, never cured; tis his minde        15

That doth afflict his body; and that warre

Quickly brings on destruction.

Q. Alex.

Whence should proceed these passions?

[IV.i.]

Ad.

    All I can gather is his banishment,

    Which, drawing something to his conscience,         20

    Makes every thing more mortall.

Q. Alex.

    Advice and sufferance is a ready cure

    For these distempered passions; and might I

    But see him, I would boldly tender them.

Ad.

    Your Highnesse may; for now he's comming forth     25

    To change the ayre, not his affliction.


    Enter Pheroas sicke in a chayre.


Phe.

    Leave me, O leave me to my selfe, that I may thinke

    Upon the tedious houres I've yet to live.

    O, what a journey hath that man to heaven,

    Whose conscience is opprest with injury;         30

    Sinne, like so many pullies hanging by,

    To draw the soule still downward: Herod; O Herod.

Q. Alex.

    Ha, what's this? sure I must sound his deeper:

    How fare you Sir?

Phe.

    O Madam, Madam; I am full of miseries.         35

[IV.i.]

Q. Alex.

Discourse with Patience; she will comfort you.

Phe.

Patience? there is a worme hath bitten Patience off;

And, being entred, sucks my vitalls up.

Herod, loath'd Herod: O credulous Pheroas!

Q. Alex.

Why doe you call on Herod?                                          40

Phe.

Nothing now:

Was't not a strange thing, that he kild his wife?

Q. Alex.

Who doe you meane, Marriam?

Indeed 'twas easily done; but soundly sworne to.

Phe.

O, I feele a dagger.                                               45

Q. Alex.

Let not her name offend you; she deserv'd

A death more horrid, and her end was just:

O Pheroas, I hated her for that act

More then the scriech-owle day; and would my selfe

Have beene her executioner; had not law                            50

Stept in twixt me and anger.

---

44. 'twas) Quarto: t'was

[IV.i.]

Phe.

> O Madam, y'are deceiv'd; meerely deceiv'd:
>
> I have a conscience tels me otherwise.
>
> O my sinnes leave, torment me not within,
>
> Nor raise this strange rebellion:  harke, they cry          55
>
> Judgement upon a wretch; that wretch am I.

Q. Alex.

> This savors of distraction.

Phe.

> A hall, a hall; let all the deadly sinnes
>
> Come in and here accuse me:  Ile confesse,
>
> Truth must no longer be obscur'd:  why so;          60
>
> All things are now prepar'd; the Judge is set,
>
> And wrangling pleaders buzzing in his eares,
>
> Makes Babel no confusion.

Q. Alex.

> Whom doe you see Sir?

Phe.

> Feare and a guilty conscience; nay, what's more,          65
>
> See where proud Herod and pale Envy sits;
>
> Poore Marriam standing at the barre of death,
>
> And her accuser I, falsly opposing her.

Ad.

> Let not your passion worke thus.

Q. Alex.

> Give him leave; passion abates by venting.          70

[IV.i.]

Eue.

    This is strange meditation.

Phe.

    I doe confesse before the Mercy-seate

    Of men and angels, I slew Marriam;

    'Twas I accus'd her falsly, I subornd,

    Strucke her toth'heart with slander; but her foes    75

    Shall follow after when the hubbub comes

    And overtakes  me downward, downe below,

    In hell amongst the damned.

Q. Alex.

                   Gentle Sir,

    Name them which thus seduc'd you.

Phe.

    Pardon mee,    80

    I dare not, nor I may not; you may guesse,

    Their characters are easie; for my selfe,

    Let mine owne shame sleepe with me; I confesse,

    Marriam was chast as faire, all good, all vertuous.

Q. Alex.

    But yet, shee's dead.    85

Phe.

    So are my joyes and comforts:  O, till now

    I had cleane lost my selfe; and as a man

    Left in a wildernesse, findes out no path

[IV.i.]

    To carry him to safety; so was I

    Distract, till this was utter'd.                90

Q. Alex.

    You have divulg'd a mystery, whose truth

    Shall sprinkle blood through all Jerusalem.

    O me, poore innocent Marriam, let thy soule

    Looke downe on my revengement; for thy sake,

    I will forget all greatnesse; faith I will.        95

    Sir, I doe wish you may dye happy now;

    Your free confession is a sacrifice.

Phe.

    Madam, I thanke you; and believ't for truth,

    The hurly burly which but late I had

    Is now appeas'd; Truth's a brave secretary.     100

    I could not rest before; yet now I feele

    A calmenesse overspread me; and my minde,

    Like a decayed temple new adorn'd,

    Shewes, as it nere was sullied.

Q. Alex.

    Y'are happy Sir.                      105

Phe.

    Madam, I am; for, with this peace of minde,

    I finde my breath decaying; yet before

    I take this long last journey, one thing more

    I must disclose; then, all is perfitted.

    Wife, reach me the violl standing in my study,    110

[IV.i.]

    Of which I was so carefull, and did binde

    Your selfe by oath to looke to: goe, away;        Exit Adda.

    Tis a new birth that Villany would bring forth.

Eue.

    More mischiefes yet in hatching?

Q. Alex.

    These actions leade you on to happinesse;        115

    And for the penitent man, remission stands

    Ready to fold him in her christall armes:

    Yet noble Pheroas, make me so much blest,

    To know who plotted Marriam's tragoedy.

Phe.

    Name it no more; ope not my wound afresh;        120

    Least, in th'incision, I should bleed to death:

    I have too much upon me; adde to fire,

    Not oyle, but water;* seas will not raise his care,

    Whose ship lies sanded on the hill Despaire.

Ad.

    Sir, here's the violl.        Enter Adda.

Phe.

    Here's a little compasse; but a mighty sound:        126

    And in this little thimble, lies strange villany.

    Madam, 'twas once prepared for the King;

    And he from me deserv'd it; not from him

    That bought it to destroy him: but Ile shew        130

    Mercy to my tormenters.

[IV.i.]

Q. Alex.

                    And those deeds

    Argue a pious nature.

Phe.

                    If they doe;

    Then thus I will expresse them:  Wife, by all

    The ties that I can challenge, or intreate

    By oath, by faith, by love and loyall duty,                    135

    I binde thee keepe this glasse till I be dead;

    But, once departed, spill it on the ground,53

    Where nere treads living creature; and (though urg'd)

    Deny thou ever sawst it; yea, though death

    Be threatned to confesse it:  this perform'd,                    140

    My peace is made with all things.

Ad.

    By all the bonds of love and faith I will.

Phe.

    Then Herod doe thy worst; I am beyond

    The reach of all thine envy; peace dwels heere;

    And quiet Slumber sits upon mine eyes:                    145

    I have no racks nor batteries now within,

    As earst I had when I was troubled:

    My nummed feete which late so leaden were,

    I could not stand nor walke; have now such warmth,

    That I can travell unto Paradise;                    150

    And, with spread armes, incircle mercy to me:

[IV.i.]

    I that accus'd the Queene, accuse my selfe,

    And on her altar lay my bleeding heart;

    Where I have found such mercy in my truth,

    That Marriams selfe hath got me happy pardon:       155

    For which deare sweet I thanke thee:  now I come,

    My life hath runne its circle, and's come round;

    Mount soule to heaven; sinke sins unto the ground.*     Dies.

Ad.

    O, he is gone, his life is withered:

    What shall become of me?  I'm lost for ever.       160

    My Lord, my Husband; O, my Pheroas;

    Lift up those eyes, they are too soone obscur'd

    From her, that as her life did tender thee.

Q. Alex.

    Have patience; tis a fruitlesse dialogue,

    Since to the dead you speake; withdraw him hence,     165

    His conscience is unburthened, he secure

    On his long journey wander'd; and beleev't,

    The causers of his woe shall follow him;

    By all that's good they shall; second me Fate,

    And let revenge once murder cruel hate.     Exit Alex. & Ad.

Eu.

    No, Ile prevent you, Salumith shall know,      171

    All your designes, and how your actions goe.     Exit eunuch.

------------

157.  its) Quarto:  it's

[IV.ii.]


[Scoena 2.]


Enter Herod [,] Niraleus, Animis, Hillus, and attendants.


Her.

Where is Niraleus? what, have you tane survey

Of all the holy building? May't be said,

Herod in it hath out-gone Salomon?

Nir.

Dread Sir, it may: nay and so farre out-gone,

As sunshine petty starre-light.

Her.

                              Come discourse                    5

The manner of the building.[54]

Nir.

                         Briefly thus,

The Temple which King Salomon set up,

In honor of the God of Israel,

(Being by your great Mightinesse defac'd)

Is thus by you restor'd. The generall frame,          10

In height, in breadth, in length, is every way

Fully an hundred cubits; and besides,

Twenty lies hid in the foundation:

The matter is white marble; every stone

Twelve cubits broad, and eight ith' outward part;     15

[IV.ii.]

So curiously contriv'd, that not a hayre

Differs in all the building:  every gate

Is clos'd in gold, and so enchast and set

With precious stones; that never, till this day,

Saw mortall man so rich a jewelry:                                    20

The tops and thresholds, silver; and each barre

Studded with knobs of shining diamonds.

Close to the holy building, stands a court

Of square proportion; every way stretcht out

Seaven hundred and twenty cubits:  all the wall            25

Is made of massie silver, and adornd

With pillars of white marble; from whose base

Toth' top are forty cubits; and thereon

Mounted such curious walkes and galleries,

That thence you may behold the fishes dance*                  30

Within the River Cedron:* all the floore

Is pav'd with marble, touch, and ivory;

And on the golden gate, is finely wrought

A flaming sword; which, by inscription,

Threats death to all dare enter.

Her.

                           What's within?                      35

Nir.

Within this court, is fram'd a curious vine

Of perfect gold; the body and large armes,

Of shining gold, brought from Arabia:*

[IV.ii.]

The sprayes and lesser branches, are compact

Of Ophyr* gold; more red and radiant:                    40

The tops and twines, whereon the clusters hang,

Are yellow gold; wrought in Assyria:

The fruit it selfe is christall; and so joynd,

That when the sunne looks on them, they reflect

And vary in their colours severall wayes,                 45

According to their objects.  To conclude;

Such art, such wealth, and wonder in the frame

Is joynd and wed together; that the world

Shall never see it equal'd:*  but this truth

Shall still hang on it as a prophesie:                    50

Blush Art and Nature; none below the sunne

Shall ever doe what Herod now hath done.

Her.

Enough, th'ast given me satisfaction; and forthwith,

In solemne wise Ile have it consecrate

Unto the God of Israel:  how now;                         55

Why comes our sister thus amazedly.


Enter Salumith, and the eunuch.


Sal.

Sir, I beseech you, for your royall health,

And for the kingdomes safety, you'l be pleas'd

To heare this eunuch speake; and howsoere

[IV.ii.]

Yave vow'd no more to heare conspiracies:                  60

Yet Sir, in this regard him; and admit,

He may make knowne what may endanger you.

Her.

Whence is the eunuch?

Sal.

                    Belonging to Alexandra.

Her.

Let him speake freely.

Eu.55

It pleas'd my lady Sir, this other day,                    65

(Hearing how desperately strong sicknesse rag'd

Upon Prince Pheroas) for some speciall cause

To goe and visite him; she found him pain'd,

Both in his minde and body; uttering forth

Many distracted speeches; some against                    70

Your Highnesse person, most against himselfe;

Saying, he had maliciously accus'd

The late Queene most unjustly:  in the end,

He makes his lady from his study bring

A violl fild with poyson; saying, this                     75

Was for the King prepared; and by those

That had least cause to hurt him:  when he had

View'd it, and shew'd the venome; he bequeathes

The violl to his lady; gives her charge

Of safe and curious keeping, till his eyes                 80

[IV.ii.]

    Were clos'd in death for ever; but, that done,

    To cast it forth and spill it on the ground,

    Where none that lives might know it: this scarse spoke,

    His soule forsakes his body; but the glasse

    My lady, and his sad wife doth preserve,           85

    I feare, for your destruction; Marriams soule

    Hath strong revengement promis'd.

Her.

                         Tis enough;

    Th'ast told me likely danger: Hillus with

    Your guard attach the wife of Pheroas;

    Then search the house; and whatsoere you finde     90

    Like poyson, see you bring me: Animis,

    With your guard ceaze my mother;* goe, away;

    Be carefull, & be happy.

An.

                  Doubt us not.         Ex. An. & Hil.

Her.

    Still shall I thus be hunted, and compel'd

    To turne head on mine owne blood? Is there left     95

    Nothing to guard me but my cruelty?

    Then let my passion conquer and keepe downe

    All mercy from appearing.

Sal.

                  Sir, twill be

    A royall justice in you: who not knowes

[IV.ii.]

The Lybian lyons never dare approach                        100

The walls wheron their spoiles hang; wolves we see

Fly from the sound of those drums, which we know

Are headed with their owne skins:  Sir, beleev't,

Severity brings safety.

Her.

                              Tis most true,

And I will hence begin to study it.                        105

How now, whom have you there?


Enter Hillus with his guard, bringing in Adda in a chaire.


Hil.

Sir, tis the wife of the deceased Pheroas.

Her.

By what meanes comes she thus disabled?

Hil.

By her owne fatall mischiefe:  when she saw

I did approach her dwelling; first she barres         110

All dores against my passage; then, her selfe

Mounts up into a turret, which orelookes

What ever stands about it; thence she calls,

And asks me what I came for; I declar'd

The pleasure of your Greatnesse; and with tearmes    115

Fit for her royall calling, wisht she would

Obey what I must finish:  she returnes

[IV.ii.]

    An answer like her fury; said she would

    Nor yeeld to you, nor mine authority.

    Which anger being over; she cry'd see,                    120

    Thus will I flye to Herod; and that spoke,

    Downe from the turret did she throw her selfe[56]

    As if a whirle-winde tooke her:  which perceivd,

    I made the soldiers catch her; yet the force

    Came with such deadly violence, that some                 125

    She struck dead underneath her; and her selfe

    Bruiz'd, as you see, and wounded:  by our meanes

    Hath yet so much life left, as may resolve,

    What we cannot discover.

Her.

                    What of the poyson?

Hil.

    No where to be found.                                     130

Sal.

    Twas a strange desperate hazard.

Her.

                    But a toy;

    They which dare doe, dare suffer; desperate soule,

    Doe not play with more mischiefe; but confesse,

    Where is the poyson, which thy treacherous lord

    (Having for me provided) did convay                       135

    Unto thy charge and keeping.

[IV.ii.]

Ad.

                         Sir, I vow,

   There nere was any given me; neither had

   My lord a thought so odious.[57]

Her.

                      Come tis false;

   Nor can you now outstrip me; to denye,

   Is but to adde to sorrow; or confesse,            140

   Or drinke of more affliction.

Sal.

                      Madam, doe;

   It will be too apparant, trust the King;

   Ile sue and begge your safety.

Nir.

                      Tis advice

   Worthy your best imbraces.

Her.

                      Quickly speake;

   For I am sodaine in my cruelty.            145

Ad.

   What shall I speake; but, that y'are tirannous,

   Thus to compell a falshood; I protest,

   He never gave me any; nor know I

   Of any hidden poyson.

Her.

   Prepare her for the torture: shall my life      150

[IV.ii.]

    Lye in these rotten caskets, and not I

    Dare to consume or breake them?  Wretched thing,

    Ile make you speake louder then tempests doe;

    And true as oracles; or else, beleev't,        They racke Adda.

    Ile cracke your strongest heart-strings:  so, pull home;

    Stretch her out like a lutestring.             156

Ad.

    O, as y'are a king have mercy; hold, O hold.

Her.

    Speake truth, or there's no mercy; higher yet.

Ad.

    O, my weake strength cannot beare it; hold, O hold.

    I will confesse and perish.                160

Her.

    Doe it with truth there's safety, give her ease.

Ad.

    I doe confesse the poyson; that my lord

    Bequeath'd it to my keeping; that it was

    Prepar'd to kill you:  but (great Sir)

    Never by him.                       165

Her.

    Who then became the author?

Ad.

    Sir, 'twas Antipater.[58]

[IV.ii.]

Sal.

                    Mischiefe on mischiefe,

How came shee by that knowledge?

Her.

    Antipater! how, from Antipater?

Ad.

    Ere his departure unto Rome, he came              170

    And feasted with my lord; declar'd his hopes;

    And that betwixt him and the crowne, did stand

    Nothing but your weake life, and great Augustus favour:

    The latter got; the first he said should fall,

    And vanish in a moment; to which end,               175

    He had prepar'd that poyson; and besought

    My lord to keepe it safely; for he meant

    At his returne to use it.

Her.

    Can you tell by whose meanes he attaind it?

Ad.

    He bought it of the Jew Achitophel.                180

Her.

    What did you with that poyson?

Ad.

    As my dead lord commanded; on the grownd

    I cast most part thereof; only some drops

    Left in the viols bottome, with the glasse,[59]

[IV.ii.]

(At her most strong intreaty) I bestow'd          185

On the Queene Alexandra.

Her.

                              Take her downe;

This at the first had eas'd your misery:

Ha Sir, Antipater; all this Antipater?

O heaven! But tis no wonder.

Nir.

                              Yes, that truth

Should thus come forth by miracle; till now          190

Mischiefe hath gone safe guarded:  but, I hope,

Your Highnesse will make use on't.

Her.

                              Doubt me not.


Enter Animis, bringing in Alexandra, Achitophel, & Disease.


Here comes my second trouble:  what the Jew?

You have prevented sending for:  false Queene,

That hast disgrac'd thy sexe with cruelty.          195

What poyson's in your keeping?

Q. Alex.

                              Not any Sir.

Her.

Not any:  impudent?

[IV.ii.]

Ad.

O Madam, tis

Too late now to excuse it; paine, O paine,

Tirannous paine hath torne all from my bosome:

The violl which I gave you, and the drops,                    200

Is that his Highnesse urges.

Q. Alex.

I do confesse them;

Heere is the violl and the drops:  from this,

What can your malice gather?

Her.

That your intent

Was, therewith to destroy me.  O, you gods!

What's life, when this can take it?  This, this drop;        205

This little paltry nothing.

Q. Alex.

Sir, tis false [:]

I never did intend your injury.

Sal.

What not intend it?  Blushlesse impudence!

Q. Alex.

If you be made my judge, I know I'm then

Worse then all feare can make me.

Her.

Y'are indeed                          210

[IV.ii.]

    A mischiefe too long growing.  Sirrah, Jew;

    Was this your composition?

Ach.

                  'Twas a worke

    My art brought forth; but never did my thought

    Touch at your Highnes.

Her.

              Who made you to prepare it?

Ach.

    The Prince Antipater.                          215

Sal.

    Villaine, th'art damn'd for that discovery.

Ach.

    No matter; Ile have royall company.

Her.

    And sirrah, you had a finger in this worke too.

Dis.

    No truly my Lord, I durst not dip my finger in your dish,

    after great men is alwayes good manners.          220

Nir.

    Then you knew it was prepared for the King.

Dis.

    Alas, I knew my maister had nothing too deare for his

    Grace, and my Lord Antipater I know gave a good price for it.

Her.

    Was this poyson then prepar'd for me?

[IV.ii.]

Dis.

O Sir, by all likelihood; for ever your physitian is like

your hauke; the greater the fowle is that he kils, the          226

greater is still both his reward and reputation.

Her.

Tis true, and you shall both finde it:  goe, hang up that

peasant presently; and then cast him into Silo.

Dis.

Who me, hang up me?  that cannot be good payment.          230

Sal.

Why foole?

Dis.

Because I shall never be able to acknowledge satisfaction.

Her.

Away with him; and for that treacherous Jew,          Ex. Dis.

And you false-hearted Madam, both shall tast

Of that you would have tendred; equally          235

Divide that bane into two cups of wine,

And give it them to drinke off; tis decreed,

What was prepar'd for me, shall make you bleed.[60]

Q. Alex.

Tis welcome Sir; a sodaine death, I know

Is terrible and fearfull; but indeed,          240

To those which doe attend it, and doe stand

Constantly gazing on it; who doe live,

Where it scarres none but cowards; those can meet,

[IV.ii.]

    And kisse it as a sweet companion:

    Tis unto those a bugbeare, who do thinke                    245

    Never on heaven, but for necessity.

    Your tyranny hath taught me other rules;

    And this guest comes long lookt for:  heere's a health

    To all that honor vertue; let suffice,           Drinks the poyson.

    Death doth oretake; but it doth not surprize.               250

Ach.

    Well Madam, I must pledge you; yet before,

    Ile doe the King some service:  I confesse,

    I did compound the poyson; 'twas prepar'd

    To kill your Majesty; the plot was laid

    Both by Antipater and Salumith:[61]                         255

    They equally subborn'd me; each bestow'd

    Reward upon mee, and encouragement:

    'Twas they which made me to accuse the Queene,

    I must confesse unjustly; they, long since,

    Have shar'd you and the kingdome:  that tis true,           260

    Be this last draught my witnesse; for no slave

    Madly will carry falshood to his grave.          Drinks the poyson.

Sal.

    But thou dost, and it will damne thee.

Her.

                                Say not so;

---

258.   'Twas) Quarto:  T'was

[IV.ii.]

I know this smoake will kindle, and my care

Must now prevent my danger.  Animis,                    Exe. Ani. & Sal.

Guard you my sister safely:  Hillus, cause                          266

Those bodies to be buried:  you Niraleus,

Shall make for Rome with all speed; thence, bring backe

That false, ingratefull, proud Antipater:

Carry the matter close, but cunningly:*62                            270

For that poore soule, bid our phisitians

With all care to respect her;63 for tis she

That onely can accuse our enemies.

Thus runnes the wheeles of state, now up, now downe;

And none that lives findes safety in a crowne.               Exeunt.


[Enter Josephus as they are leaving.]


                            Dumbe shew.

Enter at one doore, Augustus triumphant with his Romans;

at another Antipater:  he kneeles and gives Augustus letters;

which lookt on, Augustus raises him, sets him in his chayre,

and crownes him, sweares him on his sword, and delivers him

letters:  then, enter Niraleus, he gives Antipater letters;

hee shewes them to Augustus; then, imbracing, they take

leave and depart severally.

Jose.

Once more, I must intreat you to bestow                             276

Much on imagination; and to thinke,

[IV.ii. & V.i.]

    That now our bastard hath attain'd the top

    And height of his ambition:  you have seene

    Augustus crowne him; all his great requests         280

    Are summ'd and granted:  therefore, now suppose

    He is come home in triumph; all his plots

    He holds as strong as Fate is, nothing feares;

    (So brave his minde inchants him) how at last,

    He falls to utter ruine; sit, and see:         285

    No man hath power to out-worke Destinie.*        Exit.


          Finis actus quarti.

---

         Act. 5. Scoena 1.


Enter Antipater, and Niraleus.


Anti.

    O Niraleus; so liberall was the royall brested Caesar,

    As farre exceeds all thought or just expression.

    When he establisht me Judea's King,

    His bounty did so farre extend it selfe,

    That even his court appeard a paradise;         5

---

S.D. Scoena) Quarto:  Scoena.

[V.i.]

    The people like so many demi-kings;

    Himselfe, the great vice-gerent ore them all.

Nir.

    Caesar is royall, and Antipater deserving.

Ant.

    Me thinkes (as in a mirror) still I see

    Augustus dealing yellow Arabian gold          10

    Amongst the vulgar, in Antipaters name;

    So lovely were his lookes, so angel-like his words

    The very thought strikes me into a rapture:

    O, I could laugh my selfe breathlesse in conceit,

    To thinke on those faire honors we receiv'd.     15

Nir.

    Live to deserve ever.


    Enter 3. lords laughing, and pointing scornfully at

    Antipater.[64]


Ant.

    How now; what motion-mongers are these?  'Sdeath,

    what meane they?  Doe they make mee a batchellor cuckold?

    But that I would know the intent, I could be very angry:  but

    Ile not minde 'em.                20

------------

17.  'Sdeath) Quarto: S'death    18.  cuckold) Quarto: cuckond

[V.i.]

1.

    That's he was carried in triumph throu̸gh Rome.

2.

    Poore young-man, thy Greatnes must downe.

3.

    He scornd (being great) to looke on poverty;

    but now poverty scornes basenesse:  farewell.

1.

    Your Greatnesse will have a cold welcome home.       25

2.

    See how he lookes.

1.

               Pittifully pale.

1.

    I doubt hee'l runne mad.

2.

    Come, let's leave him.  Ha, ha, ha.           Exeunt.

Antip.

    Has Nature stampt me with deformity?

    Am I of late transform'd?  Am I the owle         30

    So lately made,* for birds to wonder at?  Is't so?

    I thinke I am my selfe; I have my voyce,

    My legs, my hands, my head, face, eyes and nose;

    I'm disproportion'd no way that I know of:

    Then why doe these wood-cracks* wonder at me?     35

[V.i.]

    I could be naturally vex't, and have good cause for't:

    But Ile be patient, walke, observe:  here comes a friend.


    Enter Animis, walking by Antipater.


Ani.

    My Lord;--You are undone.                      [Exit.]

Ant.

    Ha, noble Animis; what, gone so soone?           39

Ant.

    Noble Hillus.                    Enter Hillus.

Hil.

    My Lord;--Your necke is broke.              Exit.

Ant.

    Ha! whats that?  strange entertainment:  y'are undone:

    Whom should this be; for me it cannot be?  No;

    I am a king, and tis a hard matter to undoe a king.

    Pish; there's no morall in these foolish words:     45

    Your necke is broke; a banquerout's sentence.

    We are unlimited, both in wealth, and state;

    As boundlesse as the sea; freer in guift.*

    No; tis not their words can breed amazement;

    But their strange looks, gestures, and geerings at me:     50

[V.i.]

    Instruct me good Niraleus, thou art an honest man;

    How shewes this disrespect? strangely: does it not?

Nir.

    Nothing, nothing Sir; courtiers you know are apish:

    Tis onely some new project they have to entertaine you.

Ant.

    Projects for entertainment! Well, th'are strange;       55

    And I finde something troubles mee.

Nir.

    What ayle you Sir? D'yee faint? Y'are wondrous pale;

    You change colour strangely: d'yee bleed?

Ant.

    A drop; nothing, but a drop.

Nir.

    Tis ominous.       60

Ant.

    True; and I finde something that staggers me:

    I will retire my selfe from court to day.

Nir.

    Retire from court! O, name it not for shame;

    Least you incurre a publike scandall on you:[65]

    Why should you flye from that most covets you?       65

    Will you obscure your sunne-beames in their height?

    Cover your glories in their mornings rise?

---

52.  does) Quarto: doe's

[V.i.]

Those that now geered; then, will laugh outright;

When lookes can put Antipater to flight.

No, forage on; and, like a daring lion,                    70

Single your game; let not pale Feare dismay you:

Appeale for justice to heroicke Herod,

Gainst those that thus contemn'd your soveraignty:

True valour in the weakest trench doth lie;

Then beare you bravely on, and scorne to flye.              75

Ant.

Th'ast new created me:  I love this honor,

That is by merit purchas'd:  second me then;

And let the worst of fortunes fall upon me:

This guard Ile keepe; grapling this sword,

(Though wall'd with pikes) Ile beat my passage through;     80

And to great Herod make my supplication.

He that feares envy shall be sure to finde it:

But he securest, that the least does minde it.

Stay, a new onset.


Enter Animis, with a guard.


Ani.

Great Antipater.                                           85

———————

83.  does) Quarto:  doe's

[V.i.]

Ant.

    I, that sounds nobly; why not this before?

Ani.

    This cause and this authority.         Wips forth his sword.

Ant.

    What, betraid; and sleeping taken? Niraleus:

    Slaves let me goe, Ile to the King for justice:

    Ha yee caught the lambe within the lions denne?       90

    Cowardly wretches: O for my good sword,

    And liberty to gratulate your trecheries.

Nir.

    Your treasons must be first answer'd Sir;

    Til then, you must to prison.

Ant.

    Ha, Niraleus; art thou my accuser?           95

    Have I within my bosome kept a snake,

    To sting mee first?* Trecherous Lords,

    My treasons? 'gainst whom? or, by whom acted?

    Innocence protect me: guide me to Herod,

    That, to his sacred person, I may tell         100

    The injuries Antipater does suffer:

    He comes; O happy houre: justice; justice Sir.


Enter Herod, Hillus, and attendants.

[V.i.]

Her.

The justice that you merit; hence away with him.

Ant.

O sacred Herod, heare thy vassall speake:

Consider what I am; thy sonne: if my offences          105

Prove prejudiciall to thee; Ile lay my life

As foot-stoole to thy mercies: O, consider,

I never was that disobedient sonne,

That did in any thing oppose his father:

But with a greedinesse, still ranne to act,          110

Ere thy command was past: if these honours,

These titular glories, great Augustus gave me;

If these offend my Soveraigne, cut them off;

Raze them from off my head; and let me be

Any thing, but Herods scorne; no misery          115

Can worke upon me halfe that troubled griefe,

As does one frowne from those thy glorious eyes:

Let not those white haires now be staind with blood,

Blood of thine owne begetting; every drop

In me, from thee had being; canst thou be so unkind,          120

To cast thy selfe away? O sacred Sir,

I see compassion in your tender eyes;

Weeping for me, that mone your miseries.[66]

Her.

Through what a labyrinth is mercy led;

Rise in our favour evermore belov'd.          125

[V.i.]

Nir.

Rise in your favour!  O Herod be more just;

As thou art King; so be a god in justice;

The blood of babes, cryes for thine equity:

Remember but his strattagems forepast;

All which, acquitting, you are accessary.                    130

Thinke first on Aristobulus fell death;

Your two brave sonnes, and noble Josephs fall:

Next Pheroas your brother; O, your native blood:

And Alexandra, that most innocent lady;

Unjustly and untimely brought to death,                      135

All through his poysnous complots.

Her.

All these are past and cannot be recal'd.

Nir.

Let not his smooth words Sir intice you to him;

In stillest rivers are the greatest dangers:

If none of these can move you to doe justice,                140

Whose soules yet hovering still doe cry revenge;

Yet there is one whose cause must not be slipt;

Though cannons roare yet must not you be deafe;

But (like the glory you were made for) be

A king, a god in judgement, and in justice:                  145

Sonnes are no longer ours, then they are Natures;

When Nature leaves them, we may leave our claime:

Be this your warrant, justly to execute

[V.i.]

    Judgement on him, that has unjustly murdred

    Your mother,* sons, brothers, sisters:  if not for these;

    Thinke upon her as deare as was your life,          151

    Your Marriam; your innocent, chast, faire Marriam;

    By his false witnesse, turn'd to untimely dust:

    O as y'are great, be good, gracious, and just.

Her.

    All those forenamed were of no effect:          155

    My Marriam;[67] O my heart:  hence with the slave;

    Ile heare no more of his inchanting words.

Antip.

    O Herod, kingly Father.          Exit Antip. with a guard.

Her.

    Away with him; Ile blot out all affinity:

    O Niraleus, he was so deeply rooted in our love;      160

    All those and thousands more could never worke

    Me to have sent him from my presence:  but

    My Marriam; O, the very name of her

    Is like a passing-knell, to a sicke man:

    For, if to be a king, is to be wretched;         165

    Then to be meane is to be glorious:

    The thought of Marriam, like a fever burnes,

    Dissects me every nerve; I feele within

---

149.  has) Quarto:  ha's      152.  your innocent) Quarto:  you innocent

[V.i.]

    My cogitations beating, things long past

    Are now presented, now I suffer for them;          170

    I'm growne a monster, and could chase my selfe

    Out of my selfe; I'm all on fire within:

    O Marriam, Marriam, mistris of my soule;

    I shall expire with breathing on thy name:

    Thy deare remembrance burnes me:  who attends?      175

    Give me some fruit to coole me.

Nir.

    What, will you tast some sirrop, or some grapes?

Her.

    No, give me an apple.

Nir.

                    Here are faire ones Sir.

Her.

    Lend me a knife to pare it:  O Niraleus,

    I have done cruell justice; is there left           180

    A good thing to succeed me?[68]  All my sonnes,

    My brothers, sisters;[69] nay, the very last

    Of all my blood is vanisht.

Nir.

    Say not so; your childrens children live yet:

Her.

    Passing true, young Archelaus and Antipas;[70]      185

---

171.  chase) Quarto:  chafe

[V.i.]

    Bee't your charge to see them sent for home;

    Something I must act, worthy my meditation;

    Ile not live to have care dwell so neere me; one small pricke

    With this will doe it:  thus Ile trye it.[71]    Stabs himselfe.

Nir.

    Hold, in the name of wonder; what have you done Sir?    190

Her.

    Nothing but sought to ease my misery;

    A little more had done it.

Nir.

    Good Sir have patience; a surgeon there.

Her.

    Patience, thou seest I have, to kill my selfe;

    I shall ere long rest in my Marriams armes:    195

    I would not be a king another yeare,

    For both the crownes of Juda and of Rome:

    Provide my bed, I'm faint and something sicke:

    Antipater, be close, Ile sift your knavery;

    A king has eye-balls that can pierce through stone;*    200

    His very lookes, shall make the slave confesse,

    Who's just, and who's unjust:  all is not well;

    Lend me your hands, wee'l try who is the strongest;

    A wager, of us two,* I live the longest.    Exeunt.

[V.ii.]


[Scoena 2.]


Enter Antipater, Hillus and a guard.


Hil.

These are (my Lord) your lodgings; here you may

Rest at your noble pleasure; when you call,

W'are ready to attend you.

Ant.

Why tis well;

Yet, if a man should aske this chambers name,                    4

You would call it a prison.

Hil.

Tis no lesse.                    Exe. guard.

Ant.                                                        [and Hil.]

Then gentlemen I thanke you; take your ease.

Never till now hadst thou Antipater,

True cause t'account with wisedome; all thy life

Has beene but sport and tennis-play: but this,

O this is <u>serio joco</u>,* such a game,                    10

As cals thy life in question; nay, thy fame;

Thy vertue, praise, and reputation:

What art thou now? a prisoner; that's a slave:

_____

9.  Has) Quarto:  Ha's

[V.ii.]

Nay, slave to slaves; slavish extremity!

But now a king; but now a cast-away;                          15

Crown'd, and uncrown'd; and undone every way:

Where's now my hellish counsellors?  my hope?

My strong bewitcht perswasion?  Rise, O rise;

And once more shew me my deliverance:

Tut, all mute and hidden; tis the Divels tricke             20

Still to forsake men in their misery;

And I am pleas'd they doe so:  let none share

Either in my downefall, or welfare.                    Enter Animis.

Keeper, welcome:  what newes hath ill lucke now?

Ani.

Strange Sir, and heavy; Rumour saith, the King             25

Hath slaine himselfe.[72]

Ant.

Ha, cal'st thou that ill newes?

What, is he dead?

Ani.                    ~ Tis strongly so reported.

Ant.

Thou dost not mocke my fortune; prethee speake,

Speake, and speake freely; thou hadst wont to love          30

And joy in what did please me:  say; is the King dead indeed?

Ani.

Upon my life, tis firmely so reported.

─────────────

21.  Still) Quarto:  Sill

[V.ii.]

Ant.

    Excellent, excellent; noble, happy newes;

    Why, what heart could wish better?  I am traunc't

    And rapt with admiration; why, I knew           35

    Fortune durst not forsake me:  now hee's dead,

    I may say, as the Divell sayes, all's mine:

    My hopes, my thoughts, my wishes:  prethee joy

    Doe not too much orecome me:  once againe,

    Say, is he dead?  is Herod vanished?          40

An.

    Questionles, so talkes Rumour.

Antip.

                      Name it truth;

    Doe not abuse a thing so excellent:

    And now hee's dead; who thinkst thou is the King?

Ani.

    I thinke your Greatnesse only.

Ant.

                    Why, tis true;

    Exceeding true; who, but Antipater:           45

    Hath not Augustus chose me?  set the crowne

    Here?  here, my Animis?  hath not publique Rome

    Stil'd me the King of Juda?  is there left

    Any of Casmonani;[73] or the seede

    Which they doe call the holy Israel?          50

    No, I have sent them packing; th'are as dead

[V.ii.]

    As Herod and my feares are: O, my joyes,

    How nimble have you made me! To behold

    The hangman hang himselfe; would it not please

    Those that stood neere the gallowes: by my life,        55

    (Which this sweet newes hath lengthened) had I seene

    The old man kill himselfe; I thinke I should

    Have burst my sides with laughing: come, let's goe;

    Ile have the crowne imediately.

Ani.

                  Go, my Lord, whither?

Ant.

    Unto the court, the city, any where;        60

    Whither my pleasure leads me.

Ani.

                Pardon me;

    I have not that commission.

Ant.

    How; not that commission? 'Sfoot, dare any heart

    Harbor a thought 'gainst me? Come, th'art wise;

    Open thy dores unto me; I have power        65

    That knowes, and can requit thee; by this hand,

    If thou withstandst my purpose; looke to be

    Despis'd and wretched.

---

63. 'Sfoot) Quarto: S'foot

[V.ii.]

Ani.

Good my Lord, be pleas'd.

Ant.

Not to have you dispute my sufferance:

Come will you let me goe?

Ani.

Sir, I dare not.                                                70

Ant.

Expect a damned mischiefe.

Ani.

Take better thoughts,

And good my Lord conceive, this is but newes;

It my be true, or false, or any way.

Ant.

You will not let me go then?

Ani.

Would I could;

Yet if you will take patience, with all hast                   75

Ile flye unto the court:  if there I finde

The newes be firme and certaine; I'm your slave:

You shall dispose your selfe, and me and all things.

Ant.

Poxe of your purity, your ginger-bread,*

And nice, safe reservations:  but, since force                 80

Makes me obay you; goe, away, be gone;

Flye as thou lookst for favour.

[V.ii.]

Ani.

                           I am vanisht.           Exit Ani.

Ant.

    O, what a thing is man!  how quickly made

    And mar'd, and yet againe reedified,

    All with a breath; to make us know, in kings,          85

    Consists the great worke of creation:*

    Why, I was lost but now; and now againe,

    Am found as great as ever; thus can Fate

    Change and rechange at pleasure; he that would

    Have kil'd, is kil'd in killing:  foolish fiends,      90

    You are deceiv'd to leave me; I shall live

    To make you bound to mine iniquity;

    Indeed I shall; and make posterity

    Cite onely my example; then (my soule)

    Sit, and sleepe out thy dangers.              95


    Antipater sits downe and slumbers; then, enter Herod,

    Augustus, Niraleus, Archelaus, Antipas, and Hillus.


Her.

    O royall Caesar, this grace thus perform'd

    In my poore visitation; makes my soule

    A bondslave to thy vertue.[74]

Aug.

                  Tis no more

[V.ii.]

Then what your worth may challenge; onely Sir,

This violence on your person, by your selfe,                    100

Must crave my reprehension.

Her.

                    Tis but fit:

Yet royall Caesar, what should Nature doe;

When, like to me, its growne unnaturall?

Turn'd a devouring serpent; eating up

The whole frye it ingendred; nay, the armes                    105

And branches of its body.  Sir, 'twas I

That kil'd the vertuous High Priest Aristobulus;


Enter E. Aristobulus, and Q. Alexandra like ghosts.


See where he comes bright angel-like:  O stay,

Doe not afflict me further:  how he moves

Like gentle ayre about me:  see, to him,                        110

Enters his royall mother; hold, O hold;

I doe confesse my vengeance, and will shed

My life-bloud to appease you.

Aug.

                    Why, this is

But fancy which torments you; here appeares

Nothing that's strange about us.

———————

106.  its) Quarto:  it's

[V.ii.]

Her.

See my sonnes; 115


Enter P. Alexander, Y. Aristobulus, and Marriam.


My lovely boyes; tis true, I murder'd you;

Come, take revenge, and spare not:  art thou there;

O, let me flye and catch thee:  bee'st thou flame,

Blastings, or mortall sicknesse; yet I **dare**

Leape and imbrace my dearest **Marriam**: 120

Marriam, O Marriam; villaines, let me goe;

You shall not hold me from her:  O, a sword,

A sword for Heavens mercy; for, but **death**,

Nothing can joyne me to her.

Aug.

This is strange;

Nor have I seene passion more powerfull:  see you hold him **fast**.

Her.

Shall I not reach my comfort?  then, O come 126

You that my wrath hath injur'd; sticke, sticke here

The arrowes of your poyson:  so; it workes, it workes.

Nir.

A slumber overtakes him.

Aug.

Let him rest.

[V.ii.]


Enter, like ghosts, Pheroas [,] Achitophel, Disease & Tryphon.


Ant.

> Hold, O hold; whither is courage vanish't?  Poxe of feares,
>
> And dreames imaginations:  shall I turne                    131
>
> Coward whilst I am sleeping?  No, Ile laugh
>
> Even in my grave, at all my villanies:
>
> Yes, in despight of thee, and thee, and both
>
> Your damned base bravadoes:  ha, ha, ha;                    135
>
> My mountebanke and's zany!  How can hell
>
> Spare such neate skipping raskals?  What, my fine
>
> Neate shaving amorous barber!  See, I dare
>
> Face, and out-face yee all; I Death himselfe;
>
> For, none of you, but dyed most worthily.                   140
>
> Ha, I am now transfigur'd:  stand away;
>
> Accuse me not you blessed innocents:
>
> O, you doe breake my brest up, teare my soule;
>
> And burne offence to an anatomy:
>
> I know my mischiefe slew you; give me leave,                145
>
> And Ile become both priest and sacrifice:
>
> They will not have mine offering:  see, th'are gone;
>
> And I am onely fool'd with visions.
>
> Sit, and sleepe out phantasmas.

Her.

> Ha, ha, ha;

[ V.ii. ]

    This vision doth not scarre me; that you fell,         150

    'Twas justice and my vertue; all your threats

    Doe but augment my triumph:  go, pack hence;     Exe. ghosts, &

    I grieve for naught but injur'd innocence.        enter Animis.

Ani.

    Where is the King my maister?

Aug.

                      What's thy will?

Ani.

    Emperiall Sir, tis from Antipater,             155

Her.

    Antipater?  speake forth, I heare thee; that's a sound

    Ever craves mine attention.

Ani.

                  Gracious Sir,

    The rumour of your death, when it had fild

    The city; flew to him.

Her.

               Yes, and then

    How tooke he my departing?  Come, I see       160

    Strange things in thy deliverance:  speake, speake free;

    How tooke he that sad message?

Ani.

               Not toth' heart.

Aug.

    No 'twas enough the count'nance languished.

[V.ii.]

Ani.

    That was as light as any.

Her.

                On thy life

    Tell me his whole demeanour.

Ani.

                Sir, in briefe;         165

When I had told the fatall accident

Both of your wound and dying; sodaine mirth

Ranne through him like a lightning; and he seemd

Onely a flame of jest and merriment:[75]

His joy was past example; and he swore,        170

His sinnes had made him King of Israel:

What shall I say; if threatnings or reward

Could but have bought his freedome; at my choyce

Lay all my heart could number.

Her.

              Peace, no more;

I thinke what thou canst utter: O, this sonne,    175

This bastard sonne hath onely ruind me:

Hell never knew his equall; all my sinnes

Are but the seeds he planted: fie, O fie.

Aug.

Do not afflict your selfe; tis Justice now

Shall take the cause in handling: Captaines harke,    180

[V.ii.]

And harke Niraleus, doe as I command;

Be vigilant and serious:  goe, away.


Whisper, & exe. Animis, Niraleus & the guard.


Ant.

It shall be so; these visions are to me,

Like old-wives tales, or dreames of goblins;

And shall passe like them, scorn'd and jested at:                    185

Why, what to me is conscience?*  if I could

Neglect it in my whole course; shall I now[,]

Now when the goale is gotten, stand affraid

Of such poore morall shadowes?  No, tis here,

Harden'd by hell and custome which shall keepe                        190

And out-face all such battry:  I'm my selfe,

A king, a royall king; and that deare joy

Shall bury all offences:  Herod's dead;

And in his grave, sleepe my distemperance.


Enter Niraleus, Animis bearing a crowne, and a guard.


Nir.

Health to the King of Juda.[76]

Ant.

Ha, what's that?                    195

[V.ii.]

Ani.

    Long life unto the King Antipater.

[Ant.]

    Is the newes true then?  is the old man dead?

    The wretched poore old man; and, have my starres

    Made me the man I wisht for?  O, you are

    My nightingales of comfort, and shall sing          200

    Notes farre above your fortunes.

Nir.

                        Sir, hee's dead;

    And in his death hath given you all, that Rome

    Before confirm'd upon you; which we thus

    Fixe on your sacred temples; onely crave,

    You will be pleas'd (as Herod did desire)          205

    That ere you do ascend the soveraigne chayre,

    First to behold his body, and on it

    Bestow one teare or naturall sacrifice.

Ant.

    O tis a rent most ready; teares in me

    Are like showers in the spring time, ever blacke;     210

    But never farre from  sunshine:  come, I have

    A longing heart and busie thoughts, which knowes

    There's much to doe in little time:  away:

    I long to meet my glory; never hower

    Was crown'd with better fate, or stronger power.       Exeunt.

[V.ii.]

Enter Hillus, officers with the scaffold, & the executioner.

Aug.

This preparation's honest; so dispatch,                    216

And place these mortall triumphs handsomely:

Sirrah, conceale your person; let no feare

Make his feare grow too early.

Exe.

                    Tis, my Lord,

My part to couch like Mischiefe, close, but sure;          220

When I breake out I'm fatall.

Her.

                    Thou speakst truth;

Would this day did not need thee:  tis a world

To thinke how strong our cares are; and how weake

All things which doe but looke like comfort:  there's

Not left in me a shadow; not a breath                      225

Of any hope hereafter; this bastards faith,

On which so much I doted, to be lost

Thus against kinde and nature; tis a sinne,

That teares my heart in pieces.

Aug.

                    Say not so;

Tis rather comfort well discovered:                        230

But peace; see th'are approaching.          Sound trumpets.

[V.ii.]


    Enter Antipater, Niraleus, Animis, and the guard.

Nir.

    Give way, stand backe; roome for the King of Juda.

Ant.

    No, let them throng about me; and behold

    Their glory, and redeemer.  Ha; what's this? a vision?

    No; a mortall prodigie:  the King is living:  O, I'm lost

    Past hope, and past imagination; by his side        236

    The Emperour Augustus:  then I see,

    There is no way, but to destruction.

Her.

    Yes, to deserv'd destruction:  wretched thing;

    Thou scorne of all are scorned; see, I live        240

    Only to sound thy judgement:  thou, that thought'st

    To build thy throane upon my sepulchre;

    See how th'art dasht in pieces.

Ant.

                    Gracious Sir.

Aug.

    Labour not for excuses; you have runne

    A strange cariere in villany; and thrust        245

----

234.  redeemer.)  Quarto:  redeemer,      239.  deserv'd)

Quarto:  deserve

[V.ii.]

    All goodnesse from you with such violence,

    That Mercy dares not helpe you.

Ant.

                         Yet, my Lord,

    Heare mine unfaigned answere.

Her.

                        In thy brest

    Was never thing lookt like simplicity;

    Thou hast made goodnesse wretched, and defam'd        250

    All vertuous things that grac'd nobility;

    Th'ast eate my blood up; made my loathed life

    Onely a scale to reach confusion;

    Of these things I accuse thee; this I prove

    Both by my life, my death, and infamie;            255

    And for this thou must perish:  one, call forth

    The minister of death; and in my view,

    Some minutes ere my dying; let me see

    His head tane from his body.

Ant.

                        Sir, O Sir;

    Thinke that you are a father.

Aug.

                        No, a king,           260

    And thence ordain'd for justice; to put backe

    Ought of that heavenly office, were to throw

    Mountaines ith face of Jupiter;* know y'are lost,

[V.ii.]

    Lost to all mankinde and mortality:

    Therefore to make your last houre better seeme,        265

    Then all that went before it; what you know

    Of treasons unrevealed; lay them forth:

    The worke will well become you.

Ant.

                       Is there no mercy?

Aug.

    Not upon earth; nor for Antipater.

Ant.

    Then farewell Hope for ever; welcome Death;        270

    I, that have made thee as mine instrument,

    Will make thee my companion; and, I thus

    Ascend and come to meete thee:  here I am

    A monarch over all that looke on mee,

    And doe despise what all you tremble at:        275

    Sir, it is true, I meant your tragedy;

    Did quite roote out your issue; and if life

    Had held, would have wipte out your memory:

    This I confesse; and to this had no helpe;

    But mine ill thoughts and wicked Salumiths.[77]      280

Aug.

    Was she assistant to you?

Ant.

                  Sir, shee was.

[V.ii.]

Aug.

Produce her presently.

Ani.

Sir, tis too late;

The heart-strong lady once imprisoned,

Forsooke all foode, all comfort, and with sighes,

Broke her poore heart in sunder.

Her.

And that word                                     285

Hath brought mine unto cracking; strike, O strike;

Dispatch the execution; or mine eyes

Will not continue to behold the grace

Of the revenge I thrist for.

Ant.

Feare me not;

I am as swift in my desire of death,                   290

As you are in your longings:  come, thou friend

To great mens feares, and poore mens miseries,

Strike, and strike home with boldnesse; here's a life

Thy steele may quench, not conquer; for the thought

Exceeds all mortall imitation:                         295

Greatnesse grew in my cradle;* with my blood,

Twas fed to mature ripenesse; on my grave,

It shall, to all the ages of the world,

Live in eternall dreadfull epitaphs:

[V.ii.]

    This service men shall doe me; and my name           300

    Remaine a bug-beare to ambition.  Come; I am now prepar'd.

Exe.

    Sir, will you please to kneele.

Ant.

    What to thy vildnes?  Slave, Ile stand as high

    And strong as is a mountaine; strike, or perish.

Exe.

    I cannot then Sir doe mine office.           305


    Enter Salumith betweene two Furies, waving a torch.


Ant.

    Poxe of your forme in these extremities.

    What art thou there, poore tortur'd wickednes?

    And dost thou waft me to thee?  Then, I come;

    I stoope, I fall, I will doe any thing;

    Thou  art to me as Destiny:  O stay,           310

    My quicke soule shall oretake thee:  for, but we,

    Never two reacht the height of villany.

    Strike, O strike.

Her.

                 O-o-o-


    Here the executioner strikes, and Herod dies.

[V.ii.]

Aug.

Whence came that deadly groane.

Nir.

From the King; the blow the hangman gave Antipater,                    315

Tooke his life in the instant:  Sir, hee's dead.[78]

Aug.

The gods have shewd their wonders; some withdraw

The bodies and interre them:  that;* where none

May pittie or lament him:  th'other so;

As all men may admire* him:  for the crowne,                           320

Thus I bestow it on young Archelaus:[79]

Rome makes thee King of Juda; and erects

Thy chayre and throane within Jerusalem.          Sound trumpets.

All.

Long live Archelaus, King of Jerusalem.

Arch.

I will be Caesars servant; and my life,                                325

I hope shall purge these woes from Israell.

Aug.

Tis a sweet royall promise; prosper in't;

Make Vertue thy companion:  for we see,

She builds[;] their ruines spring from tyrannie.     Exeunt omnes.

---

329.  ruines) Quarto:  ruines,

---

### The Epilogue.

Y'ave heard a tale, which not a noble eare

But has drunke with devotion; and how ere

It scant in phraze or action; yet it may

Ranke with some others, and be held a play,

Though not the best, nor worst; yet wee hope                5

It keepes the middle passage; thats the scope

Of our ambition:  but, of this w'are bold,

A truer story nere was writ, or told:*

If envy hurt it, tis our fates; and we

Begge but your hands, for the recoverie.                10

### FINIS.

---

2.  has) Quarto: ha's

NOTES TO THE INTRODUCTION

[1]F. N. L. Poynter, A Bibliography of Gervase Markham 1568?-
1637 (Oxford, 1962), pp. 2ff.

[2]Although Poynter limits Markham's knowledge of foreign lan-
guages to French, Italian, and Latin, other biographers, namely Sir
Clement R. Markham ("Gervase Markham," DNB, XII, 1937, p. 1051) and
A. C. Dunstan (Examination of Two English Dramas: 'The Tragedy of
Mariam' by Elizabeth Carew; and 'The True Tragedy of Herod and
Antipater, with the Death of Faire Marriam' by Gervase Markham and
William Sampson--Königsberg, 1908--p. 51), say that Markham knew
Spanish also and perhaps Dutch.

[3]Poynter, pp. 8, 11, and 13. For speculation that Markham was
the rival poet of Shakespeare's sonnets, see Robert Gittings,
Shakespeare's Rival (London, 1960); F. G. Fleay, A Biographical
Chronicle of the English Drama 1559-1642 (London, 1891), II, 59; and
Sidney Lee, A Life of William Shakespeare (London, 1908), p. 108.

[4]Dodsley's Old English Plays, ed. William Hazlitt (London, 1875),
X, 111.

[5]Poynter, pp. 4, 21, 28-29. Markham's identity has been the
subject of some debate. C. W. Wallace (Shakespeare Jahrbuch, XLVI,
1910, pp. 345ff.) raises the question of whether Gervase Markham the

playwright was the same man as Gervase Markham the horseman. J. Q. Adams, Jr., (see note 17 below) doubts that there were two different men; but G. E. Bentley, in The Jacobean and Caroline Stage (Oxford, 1941), IV, 732-734, suggests that there may even have been a third Gervase Markham. Yet Poynter sees no reason to believe that the author of our play was not the author of the horsebooks.

[6]Even this fact has been questioned by the author of the DNB's "Corrections and Additions" concerning Sampson. According to the revised account of his life, Sampson was born c. 1600 and died c. 1656. Moreover, he was not one of the Sampsons of Nottinghamshire. (See Corrections and Additions to the DNB--Boston, 1966--pp. 176f.) It may be difficult, however, to imagine Sampson the dramatist being born as late as 1600 and revising Herod and Antipater before 1622 (see below, section IV). For the original account by Lee, see "William Sampson," DNB (Oxford, 1937), XVII, 722-723.

[7]W. W. Greg, A Bibliography of the English Printed Drama to the Restoration (Oxford, 1939-1960), II, 980.

[8]Silbermann (p. 33) explains the discrepancy of the dates (1558 for Morwyng and 1559 for Lepusculus) by arguing that Morwyng published in 1558 only part of his work, for which he was not indebted to Lepusculus. Then, after 1559, he supplemented his history by translating Lepusculus and published the augmented volume without changing the original title page.

[9]This list is given by Valency on pp. 291-292.

[10]Caius Sallustius Crispus, The two most worthy and notable histories, the Conspiracie of Cateline and the Warre which Jugurth maintained, etc., trans. Thomas Heywood (1608-09), STC 21625. Markham and Sampson may have known an earlier play, now lost, called Jugurth, King of Numidia. G. F. Reynolds (note 60 below) mentions the play (p. 26) and says that although it was not licensed until 1624, it was by then an "old play" and may have been written as early as 1600.

[11]For a few examples in Herod and Antipater, see I.ii.35; II.i.216f.; IV.ii.104; and V.i.139. The Senecan style may also be found in the bombast of some of the poetry.

[12]See I.iv.78 and 88; II.i.107; II.i.544; and IV.i.69. For examples of such warnings in Seneca, cf. Hippolytus, 11. 129-132; and Hercules Oetaeus, 11. 275-277. On the stoicism see also note 33 below.

[13]For the use of the nuntius, see I.iii.230ff.; II.i.481ff.; IV.ii.6ff.; and IV.ii.109ff.

[14]I.iii.373; see also 11. 361-364. For monologues where evil is planned in Seneca, see Agamemnon, esp. 11. 44-52; Thyestes, 11. 176ff.; Hercules Oetaeus, 11. 256ff.; Hercules Furens, esp. 75-122; and Medea, 11. 1ff. The Furies are summoned in Thyestes, 11. 250-252; Hercules Furens, 11. 86-88; and Medea, 1. 13.

[15]The similarity between Antipater's first long soliloquy
(I.iii.409-415) and that by Gloucester (Richard III, I.i.32-35) has
been noted by Dunstan (note 2 above), p. 83; and by Marcus Landau,
"Die Dramen von Herodes und Mariamne," Zeitschrift f. vergl.
Literaturgeschichte (Weimar, 1896), N. F., IX, 187. Furthermore,
Poynter (Bibliography, p. 56) sees allusions to the murder scene in
Macbeth (I.v.41-55; II.i.33f.) in Antipater's speech (I.iii.361-365;
346-349) and to Hamlet's "What a piece of work is man" (II.ii.315)
in Antipater's statement of V.ii.83. For the lines from Richard III
and Macbeth, see the Notes of Explanation and Comparison below, p. 197
and p. 193.

[16]For the reference to the Herodias see the epistle to Maister
Francis Darlow at the beginning of The Second and Last Part of The
First Booke of the English Arcadia. By G. M. (London, 1613)
[STC 17352].

[17]"Every Woman in her Humor and The Dumb Knight," MP, X
(1913), 427ff. Adams, however, not aware of the 1613 reference to
Herodias, argues for 1621 as the date of composition of Herod and
Antipater.

[18]"Recent" here is meant to designate events no more distant in
time than the War of the Roses. For Jacobean plays of either the
"foreign" or the "ancient" variety (or both), see Fletcher (and
Massinger?), Sir John van Olden Barnavelt (1619); Chapman, Chabot,
Admiral of France (c. 1621. later revised by Shirley); Massinger, The

Maid of Honour (c. 1621?); Lodowick Carlell, Osmond, the Great Turk (1622?); and Massinger, The Bondman (1623).

[19] Henry W. Wells, Elizabethan and Jacobean Playwrights (New York, 1939), p. 98. For the idea that the chronicle play spent itself, see Wells, p. 97.

[20] Wells (p. 98) marks the end of the great chronicle wave with Shakespeare's Henry V in 1600.

[21] The process was started in May, 1603, when the Lord Chamberlain's Company was re-designated as The King's Men. For an account of the new patents of the other companies, see Glynne Wickham, Early English Stages 1300 to 1660 (New York, 1963), Vol. II, Part I, 90f.

[22] On this point see Wells (note 19 above), p. 250; and Wickham, p. 94. The latter especially laments the decay of the drama under the new control. But see his suggestion (p. 90) that James's new patents gave the players security against those who opposed the drama.

[23] Nothing, however, came of the episode, and James finally pardoned the offenders. (For an account see Bentley--note 5 above-- IV, 874-875.) It was certainly not unreasonable of James to be disturbed by such a bold allusion to his failure. Even Elizabeth, far more successful as a ruler, had been sensitive to Shakespeare's Richard II, thinking her circumstance reflected in that play.

[24]According to Wickham (p. 105), this method of allegory was one of long standing when A Game at Chess appeared (1624).

[25]Critics have argued for such extended parable in each of the plays, save one, listed in note 18 above. Regarding these possibilities, see Bentley's comments on the plays. The exception is Sir John van Olden Barnavelt. While no analogue has been found in this play, Bentley wonders if Raleigh's circumstance might not be reflected in the fallen Dutchman's (Bentley, III, 417).

[26]On Herod's foreign birth, see note 24 (on p. 219 below) of the Appendix Concerning Sources.

[27]Robert Cecil, Earl of Salisbury, had been James's Lord High Treasurer and Secretary of State. Robert Carr was created Viscount Rochester in 1611 and then Earl of Somerset in 1613. George Villiers was made Earl of Buckingham in 1617; in 1619 he became marquis; and 1623 duke.

[28]Godfrey Davies, The Early Stuarts 1603-1660 (Oxford, 1937), p. 19.

[29]Although Lady Somerset was pardoned in July, 1615, she and her husband were not released from the Tower until January, 1622. Somerset did not receive his final pardon until 1624. See S. R. Gardiner's life of Carr in the DNB, III, 1085; and Bentley, V, 1090.

[30]Davies, p. 21.

[31]On Raleigh's death see Davies, p. 53. Bacon's fall, brought about when Parliament charged him with accepting bribes in chancery suits, is ironic considering that he had helped prosecute both Raleigh and the Earl of Suffolk (Lord High Treasurer), who fell in 1619. For impeachments during James's last decade, see S. R. Gardiner, The First Two Stuarts and the Puritan Revolution (New York, 1893), p. 36.

[32]The technique is so described by Felix E. Schelling, Elizabethan Drama 1558-1642 (New York, 1910), II, 35.

[33]On the Jacobean idea that the world was decaying, see Irving Ribner, Jacobean Tragedy (London, 1962), pp. 5-6. With such a pessimistic outlook, it can be easily seen why the Jacobeans embraced stoicism as the "dominant philosophy" of the era. The influence of this philosophy appears throughout Herod and Antipater in the numerous speeches where characters meet death with acceptance and fortitude. Also stoical are the warnings against passion, such as that by Alexandra (I.iv.78) and that by Antipater (II.i.544). For more data on stoicism in Jacobean tragedy, see Una Ellis-Fermor, The Jacobean Drama: An Interpretation (London, 1936--reprinted 1964), pp. 20-21; and Michael Higgins, "The Development of the 'Senecal Man,'" RES, XXIII (1947), 24-33.

[34]In the first act alone, for example, see I.iii.120; I.iii.393; I.iv.46-49; and I.v.107. Consider also the many references, both literal and figurative, to poison throughout the play.

[35]The same unusual comparison is developed throughout Cyril Tourneur's The Revenger's Tragedy (1607) and appears occasionally in his The Atheist's Tragedy (1611). In the former play see I.i.71f.; I.iv.1-3; I.iv.66; IV.i.52f.; and IV.iv.152f. In the latter see IV.iii.130f. and 135f.; and V.i.92-96.

[36]"Alexandra is not a very convincing figure," says Dunstan (note 2 above), p. 87. He too finds her nature too changeable.

[37]This idea of history was more characteristic of Elizabethan thought than of the skeptical view of many Jacobeans. On Elizabethan historiography see Irving Ribner, The English History Play in the Age of Shakespeare (Princeton, 1957), pp. 20, 24.

[38]See I.iii.99 and II.i.394. Marriam does slip once when she says, "O you gods" (I.iv.112).

[39]The "hellish counsellors" of the dumb shows, although seen only by Antipater, still leave him tangible scrolls of paper. The ghosts, seen only by Herod and Antipater, may be taken to be imaginary, as may the Furies, since no one seems to notice them but Antipater.

[40]The reconciling of the physical and spiritual realms was a difficult problem for a great many of the Jacobean playwrights. Una Ellis-Fermor (note 33 above) has written: "The visible is no longer either the image or the instrument of an invisible world [in the Jacobean drama], but exists in and per se as an alternative truth in conflict with the other and offering a rival interpretation of

phenomena.  So marked is this divergence that there is hardly a dramatist who can bring the two together" (p. 17).

[41]The events leading to Herod's discovery are these:  Pheroas, troubled by his part in Marriam's death, reveals the poison plot against Herod to Alexandra.  The eunuch overhears and runs to tell Salumith, not because he wishes to save Herod or the kingdom, but for clearly selfish motives.  Salumith then goes to Herod, again for selfish reasons, hoping to hide her part in the plot by betraying Adda.  Adda then confesses, revealing Antipater's guilt.  The discovery is thus too far removed from Pheroas to be the direct result of his confession.  And because the eunuch happens to overhear, we regard the discovery as mostly accident.

[42]In asserting his will to be supreme, Antipater resembles D'Amville, the title-figure of Tourneur's The Atheist's Tragedy.  What Ribner says about D'Amville (Jacobean Tragedy, p. 87) fits Antipater exactly:  "He believes that by his own human will and the power of his mind he can manipulate the world and other men to his advantage."

[43]In the medieval drama the recurring character named Herod actually represents three different historical Herods.  The first is Herod the Great, who killed the children when the three kings deceived him (Matt. ii.1-12, 16).  He appears in the following plays:  Towneley XIV and XVI; York XVI, XVII, and XIX; Chester VII and X; Ludus Coventriae XVII and XIX; the Coventry Pageant of the Shearmen and Taylors; and the two Digby plays--Herod's Killing of the Children, sc. 1 and 4; and Mary Magdalene, Part I, sc. 4, though the references to

Tiberius and Pilate in the last play (lines 163, 213, and 226--
cf. Luke iii.1) indicate that this Herod was confused with the
tetrarch (see below).

The second Herod is Herod Antipas, the tetrarch, son of Herod
the Great. He imprisoned and beheaded John the Baptist (Luke iii.
19-20; ix.9; Matt. xiv.1-12; and Mark vi.14-29) and also examined
Jesus for Pilate (Luke xxiii.6-12). He appears in York XXXI; Chester
XVI; Ludus Coventriae XXIX and XXX; and the Digby Mary Magdalene,
Part II, sc. 29.

The last is Herod Agrippa, the king who troubled the early
Christians (Acts xii.1) and who was finally struck down by an angel
(Acts xii.23). This is probably the dying Herod represented in Ludus
Coventriae XIX and is possibly the same in Chester X and Digby Herod's
Killing of the Children, sc. 4.

There is no evidence in the plays, however, that the medieval
dramatists bothered to distinguish between these different historical
figures. They certainly did not in regard to characterization, for
from one play to the next--whatever the subject matter--Herod seems
to be essentially the same personage. See R. E. Parker, "The
Reputation of Herod in Early English Literature," Speculum, VIII
(1933), 60-61; and Warren E. Tomlinson, Der Herodes-Charakter im
englischen Drama (Leipzig, 1934), p. 14.

In the following composite portrait of the medieval Herod, I
emphasize those traits which appear in some form in Markham and
Sampson's Herod.

[44]For this see Coventry _Pageant of the Shearmen and Taylors_, lines 777, 801-802; Digby _Mary Magdalene_, line 186; Chester VIII, 374; X, 117; Digby _Herod's Killing of the Children_, line 365; Towneley XIV, 387, 429; and XVI, 148, 230.

[45]Towneley XVI, 163-171.

[46]Chester VIII, 136.

[47]It is difficult to find a generic name to describe all of the medieval plays in which Herod appears. The term "mystery" play, used here for this purpose, hopefully will be allowed to include the two Digby plays, for which the terms "cycle" play and "Corpus Christi" play are obviously unsatisfactory. _Mary Magdalene_ is the hardest to classify, since it combines elements of the "miracle" and the "morality" plays.

[48]Herod reacts in this manner in Towneley XVI, 261-264, 474-475; York XVII, 189-190, 205; Chester VIII, 386-389; Ludus Coventriae XIX, 164-167; Digby _Mary Magdalene_, 201-202 (see also 1285-87); and Coventry _Pageant of the Shearmen and Taylors_, 814-816.

[49]For this ruse see York XVII, 121-203; and Chester VIII, 350-371; and to a lesser extent Ludus Coventriae XVII, 176-191. For more of Herod's deception see Towneley XIV, 387-504; and Coventry _Pageant of the Shearmen and Taylors_, 642-675.

[50]The medieval Herod likes to call people liars, especially when they tell him of the prophecies of Christ. See York XIX, 119,

125, 268; Towneley XIV, 265, 457; XVI, 163, 225; Chester VIII, 217, 236, 275. Cf. Markham and Sampson's Herod, II.i.556; and IV.ii.138.

[51]See Towneley XVI, 253-261; York XVII, 137-144, 181-190; XIX, 147-160; Chester X, 126-133; and Digby Mary Magdalene, 193-201. Cf. Herod and Antipater, I.iii.98; I.iii.202; and II.i.348.

[52]See York XIX, 136-138; Towneley XIV, 469-480. Cf. Herod and Antipater, I.iii.1ff.; I.v.29, 33ff.; and II.i.545-553.

[53]The advancement is understandable, and we cannot argue from it that Markham and Sampson were better dramatists than the creators of the medieval Herod. We can say only that the different playwrights had different intentions. Other factors certainly involved are the scope of the different plays--i.e., the extent of the development of each character--and the historical events dramatized. Also significant are the sources available to the playwrights. The medieval writers must have relied on the brief portraits of Herod in the Bible, since Josephus says nothing of Herod's dealings with Christ. Markham and Sampson, dramatizing the Marriam story, may have read the long psychological study of Herod given by Josephus.

[54]Tomlinson, p. 35, notes these methods of the earlier Herod.

[55]Coventry Pageant of the Shearmen and Taylors, 490-491.

[56]York XVI, 16-20; XXXI, 270-271; Towneley XIV, 35-36; Coventry Pageant of the Shearmen and Taylors, 507-513, 643; Digby Mary Magdalene, 153-155; and Ludus Coventriae XVII, 4-5, 9, 69-70, 82.

[57]York XIX, 1, 76; XXXI, 146-147, 161, 175, 293, 355, 373, 403; Towneley XVI, 273, 512-513; Chester VIII, 149-150; XVI, 173; and Coventry Pageant of the Shearmen and Taylors, 676.  Both Tomlinson (pp. 24f.) and E. K. Chambers (The Medieval Stage, II, 139f.) suggest that the French enhances the effect of Herod's bombast.

[58]Herod can rise to exquisite poetry.  See, for example, his tribute to Marriam, II.i.521-543, where the rhythm of the many clauses beginning with she, punctuated by the occasional questions, recalls the flavor of some of the finest Old Testament poetry (as in the Authorized translation and others).

[59]For echoes of Edmund and Iago, see the notes to I.ii.33f.; and I.iii.371f. in the Notes of Explanation and Comparison.

[60]George Fullmer Reynolds, The Staging of Elizabethan Plays at the Red Bull Theater 1605-1625 (New York, 1940), p. 14.

[61]That the quarto was set from a prompt-copy may be indicated by some of the stage directions.  In these the words "Clap hands" (I.iii.212), "wringing her hands" (II.i.437c), and "using ambitious countenances" (II.i.637k) tell the actors how to gesture.  This information is non-essential to the reader.

[62]Reynolds (p. 109) finds enough evidence in other plays presented at the Red Bull to conclude that there must have been three doors.

[63]Dunstan (note 2 above), p. 92.

[64]Marcus Landau (note 15 above) mentions this resemblance, p. 187.

[65]Depending on how one defines _issue_. Greg (note 7 above, _Bibliography_, II, 530) indicates only one issue, apparently deciding that the four variant copies (described in the following sentences) were not sufficiently different to constitute a separate issue.

[66]For a description of all the copies, along with their present locations, see Poynter (note 1 above), pp. 64f.

[67]_Bibliography_, II, 530.

[68]I have examined Xerox copies of three of the quartos--one, with Rhodes' epistle, from the University of Michigan's microfilm; one, with Sampson's epistle, from the Huntington Library; and one "unidentified" copy from the Folger Shakespeare Library. In collating these three I have found them to be identical except for two small variants. In the Huntington copy the catchword on E2v is correctly _Lord_; in the other two copies it is incorrectly _O_. In the Folger copy on the last leaf (L4r) a single line across the page separates the final speech by Augustus from the epilogue. In the other two copies, instead of a

single line, a double line appears. Yet the rest of the type on both

of these pages, E2v and L4r, is the same in all three copies.

NOTES OF EXPLANATION AND COMPARISON

The Prologue.

1. Times...(Truth)) Cf. phrasing of Sampson's The Vow
   Breaker (1636), IV.ii.177: "Deaths eldest daughter,
   sleepe...."

I.i.

15. markes...at) One of Markham's favorite metaphors.
    Cf. A Health to the Gentlemanly Profession of Serving-
    Men (1598; STC 17140; rprt. Oxford, 1931), sig. B2r:
    "this state and profession of Seruingmen, is the onely
    marke whereat I ayme..."; The Dumb Knight in Dodsley's
    Old English Plays (London, 1875), X, 176: "hit now the
    mark / That mine ambition aims at..." In Herod and
    Antipater see further I.iii.310f. and II.i.595.

17f. And...him) Cf. Markham's Honour in his Perfection (1624;
    STC 17361), p. 23: "for now the...Irish rebels...began
    to rage like wilde Boares, and to root vp euery fruit-
    full place in that Kingdome." Cf. also Psalm lxxx.8, 13:
    "Thou hast brought a vine out of Egypt....The wild boar
    out of the wood doth root it up...."

I.ii.

18. The lives...lend) i.e., parents or children.

191

I.ii.

33f.  By Birth...true-borne) Cf. <u>King</u> <u>Lear</u>, I.ii.199:  "Let me,
if not by birth, have lands by wit."

I.iii.

13.  witnesses) either to justify the employment of suspicion
("suspect") or to affirm the evidence presented by mere
suspicion.

44.  higher) as on a rack.  Cf. IV.ii.158.

73.  hackney) tired or slow.

82.  silly) feeble.

95f.  Not...lightening) Similar advice is given to the messenger who has infuriated the Herod of York XIX, 120-122:
"Hense! tyte, but þou þe hye, / With doulle her schall
þou dye, / That wreyes hym on this wise."

98.  topsie turvie downward) Another of Markham's favorite
expressions.  Cf. <u>Devoreux</u> (1597; <u>STC</u> 19793), stanza 23;
<u>Rodomonths</u> <u>Infernall</u> (1607; <u>STC</u> 6785), stanza 97; and
<u>The</u> <u>most</u> <u>Famous</u>...<u>Historie</u>, <u>of</u>...<u>Meruine</u> (1612; <u>STC</u>
17844), p. 48.  See also <u>Herod</u> <u>and</u> <u>Antipater</u>, III.i.359.

145.  purchase) value.

182f.  To die's...it) The idea, but not the phrasing, is
similar to <u>Measure</u> <u>for</u> <u>Measure</u>, III.i.5-8:  "Be absolute
for death; either death or life / Shall thereby be the
sweeter.  Reason thus with life: / If I do lose thee,
I do lose a thing / That none but fools would keep."

203.  Y. Alex.) This heading may be an error for <u>E</u>. <u>Arist</u>.

I.iii.

Aristobulus would more naturally address Alexandra as
"Mother," while Y. Alexander whispers with Herod.

205. lose) be lost by.

223. imbosture) embossment.

265. compasse) direction or path (an archery term: see
draw in the preceding line).

336. King...Creete) Jove as a child was hidden in Crete by
Mother Earth to protect him from his father Cronus.

346-349. Last...fall) With these lines cf. Macbeth, II.i.33f.:
"Is this a dagger which I see before me...?"

352. Gyants...heaven) Zeus, with the help of Hercules, put
down the twenty-four earth-born giants, who had heaped
up mountains of rocks from which they lept into heaven.
Cf. V.ii.252f.

359. Bacchus...gods) Bastards because they were all fathered
by Zeus on mothers other than Hera, his wife.

360. worthy) one of the nine Worthies of ancient legend.
OED lists: Joshua, David, Judas Maccabaeus, Hector,
Alexander, Julius Caesar, Arthur, Charlemagne, and
Godfrey of Bouillon.

366. Which...beleeve) With this idea of an incredible, unfor-
gettable crime, cf. Seneca's Medea, 11. 45-47: "effera
ignota horrida, / tremenda caelo pariter ac terris mala /
mens intus agitat"--"Wild deeds, unheard-of, horrible,
calamities at which heaven and earth alike shall tremble,
my heart deep within is planning"; also, 11. 423f.:

I.iii.

"faciet hic faciet dies / quod nullus umquam taceat"--
"This day shall do, shall do that whereof no day shall
e'er be dumb"; and Thyestes, 11. 192f.: "age, anime,
fac quod nulla posteritas probet, / sed nulla taceat"--
"Up! my soul, do what no coming age shall approve, but
none forget." The English, as well as the Latin, is
drawn from Seneca's Tragedies, trans. Frank Justus
Miller (Cambridge, Massachusetts, 1953), I, 230-231;
I, 262-263; and II, 104-105, respectively. See Antipater
further: V.ii.91-94 and 297-299.

367f. Whereat...tyrannie) Atreus's tyranny was his serving of
the children of Thyestes (his brother and rival for the
throne of Mycenae) to him at a banquet. The playwrights
may be thinking of Seneca's Thyestes, 11. 776-788, where,
at the horror of the event, the sun reversed its course.
With this line cf. Markham's Tragedie of Sir Richard
Grinuile in The Last Fight of the Revenge, ed. Edmund
Goldsmid (Edinburgh, 1886), II, 41: "Ile make the Sunne,
for pittie backe recoyle." Further Senecan conceits are
contained in 11. 368f. of Herod and Antipater. With the
idea of the sun's falling, cf. Thyestes, 1. 51: "excidat
caelo dies"--"let day fall from heaven" (Miller's translation, II, 95-97--see note to I.iii.366 above); and
Hippolytus, 11. 674f.: "omnis impulsus ruat / aether"--
"let all the sky fall in shattered ruin" (Miller, I, 372-

I.iii.

373).  With "the heav'ns...quake," cf. Thyestes, 11. 265f.:

"fiat nefas / quod, di, timetis"--"Let a deed of guilt

be done whereat, O gods, ye are affrighted" (Miller, II,

112-113).  And with "Nature tremble," cf. "earth...shall

tremble" in the passage from Medea, 11. 45-47, already

quoted in the note to I.iii.366 above.

370.  amaz'd) in fearful stupefaction.

371f.  My...birth) Cf. Othello, I.iii.409f.:  "I have't.  It is

engend'red.  Hell and night / Must bring this monstrous

birth to the world's light."  Cf. also Seneca's Thyestes,

11. 267f.:  "...animo maius et solito amplius / supraque

fines moris humani tumet"--"some greater thing, larger

than the common and beyond the bounds of human use is

swelling in my soul..." (Miller, II, 112-113).

Dumb shew.

curranto) a dance having a running or gliding step.

376.  seaven...crosse) The seven persons seem to be Herod, Marriam,

Salumith, Joseph, Pheroas, and the two princes (cf. below,

II.i.616f.).  The two houses are those of Herod (Greek)

and the Hasmonaean house of Marriam (Hebrew, the Casmonani

of V.ii.49).  See further note 26 of the Appendix Concerning

Sources below, p. 220.

379.  broach) pierce.

382.  hunger-starved) A frequent adjective in Markham's other

works.  See Rodomonths Infernall (1607; STC 6785), stanza

I.iii.

105; The...Historie, of...Meruine (1612; STC 17844),

p. 104: "Like a hunger-starued wolfe amongest a flocke

of sheepe"; also p. 160 and p. 193 of the same work; and

The Second...Part of...the English Arcadia (1613; STC

17352), p. 57b (misnumbered 53b): "a hunger-sterued

Tyger..." But cf. Massinger and Dekker's The Virgin-

Martyr (1622), ed. W. Gifford (London, 1805), I, 79:

"When a tiger / Leaps into a timorous herd, with ravenous

jaws, / Being hunger-starved, what tragedy then begins?"

Perhaps a common influence is Seneca's Thyestes, ll. 707-

711: "ieiuna silvis qualis in Gangeticis / inter iuvencos

tigris erravit duos, / utriusque praedae cupida quo primum

ferat / incerta morsus (flectit huc rictus suos, / illo

reflectit et famem dubiam tenet)..."--"As in the jungle

by the Ganges river a hungry tigress wavers between two

bulls, eager for each prey, but doubtful where first to

set her fangs (to the one she turns her jaws, then to the

other turns, and keeps her hunger waiting)...!"

383. fasten) lay hold (to eat).

385. My...observ'd) This cynical humor recalls Seneca's

Thyestes, ll. 717f. Here the messenger reports Atreus's

slaying of Thyestes' children. The chorus asks: which

one has he killed first? The answer is: "Primus locus

(ne desse pietatem putes) / avo dicatur: Tantalus prima

hostia est"--"The place of honour (lest you deem him

I.iii.

          lacking in reverence) to his grandsire is allotted--

          Tantalus is the first victim"--the gruesome joke hinging

          on the fact that the boy, Tantalus, had been named for

          his grandfather. (So Miller explains it, II, 150-151).

403.   *Per scelera...iter*) The line is taken from Seneca's *Aga-*

       *memnon*, 1. 115: "Through crime ever is the safe way for

       crime." "Fond is the stay of sinne" (404) thus means

       "it is foolish to delay or restrain sin when sin is

       necessary."

406.   *Nec...sciunt*) This line is also from Seneca's *Agamemnon*,

       1. 259, but *scotium* is an error for *socium*: "Nor throne

       nor bed can brook a partnership" (Miller, II, 24-25).

409-415.   Whetting...delaid) With this passage cf. *Richard III*,

       I.i.32-35: "Plots have I laid, inductions dangerous, /

       By drunken prophecies, libels, and dreams, / To set my

       brother Clarence and the King / In deadly hate the one

       against the other."

413.   decreed) This word may have rimed with laid, playd, and

       delaid in the following lines.

I.iv.

1.   plot) floor-plan (for the temple). But the word seems

       intended to echo Antipater's parting remark (I.iii.414).

S.D.   ruptures) tears and holes?

14.   trophees) Evidently, his wares.

I.iv.

32. Would...face) "who would not be wearing a mask except for the fact that her face is unattractive."

39. sculpture, painting) Both of these terms may refer to applying cosmetics (see 33f. above).

42. Sambashaw) Unidentified; perhaps a humorous invention.

64. swine of us) Cf. Matthew vii.6: "neither cast ye your pearls before swine..." The allusion is one of many anachronisms.

65. arrand) thorough, genuine; perhaps with humorous implication of thoroughly bad.

81. Chid...them) Cf. Markham's Devoreux (1597), stanza 27: "a mighty Deludge...Chiding the rocks in which his waues were pent."

120f. Not...them) The promise of an unrelenting pursuit for revenge is another Senecan element of the play. Cf., for example, Hercules Oetaeus, 11. 280-282; Hercules Furens, 11. 27-29; and Medea, 11. 401-407. For similar lines in Herod and Antipater, see I.iv.86f.; and IV.i.168-170.

122. text) write.

I.v.

29. Who...cares) Dunstan (see note 2 to the Introduction), pp. 79f., compares Herod's view of kingship with the view expressed by some of Shakespeare's kings. For example, cf. Richard II, III.ii.95f.: "Say, is my kingdom lost? Why, 'twas my care; / And what loss is it to be rid of

I.v.

care?"; and 2 Henry IV, III.i.31: "Uneasy lies the head

that wears a crown." The "cares of the crown" is also a

common theme in Seneca's plays. See, for instance,

Agamemnon, 11. 57ff.

30. fluxine) flowing? (not found in OED).

90. timerous) With 11. 66-90, cf. the following passage from

Massinger and Dekker's The Virgin-Martyr, ed. W. Gifford

(London, 1805), I, 81f.:

Sap [ritius] .    ...from what country

        Wert thou ta'en prisoner...?

Slave. From Britain....

Sap.   Sirrah fellow,

        What wouldst thou do to gain thy liberty?

Slave. ...Liberty! I'd thus

        Bestride a rampire, and defiance spit

        I' the face of death, then, when the battering-ram

        Was fetching his career backward, to pash

        Me with his horns in pieces....

                what is for man to do

        I'll venture on, to be no more a slave.

Sap.   Thou shalt, then, be no slave....

                drag that thing aside,

        And ravish her [Dorothea, the virgin martyr].

Slave. And ravish her! is this your manly service?

I.v.

> A devil scorns to do it; 'tis for a beast,
>
> A villain, not a man....
>
>> do't thyself, Roman,
>
> 'Tis drudgery fit for thee.
>
> Concerning the similarity see the Introduction to the
> present play, p. x.

Finis actus primae) This should properly read primi. Similar
solecisms occur at the end of the second and third acts.

II.i.

18. Insolent...owne) Cf. Markham's reply in a letter to his
uncle, who had called him a "lyinge Knave": "but for
'lyinge knave' w$^{th}$ him dwell it w$^{ch}$ unjustly gave it me"--
quoted by J. H. H. Lyon in A Study of The Newe Metamorphosis (New York, 1919), p. 127 n.

27-29. Come...utterd) Cf. II Peter ii.22: "The dog is turned
to his own vomit again." See also Henry V, III.vii.
68f., where the Dauphin renders the same in French.

42. (this)) Evidently accompanied with a gesture.

64. misprision) both misunderstanding and scorn.

88. crudulous) Intended for credulous, either a misprint
or a nonce spelling not in the OED.

93. perpetrate) Possibly the line means, sarcastically:
"Do you act in such a way as to bring about my benefit?"

122. rhapsodie) mass effusion?

178-181. Should...them) Cf. Markham's Tragedie of Sir Richard

II.i.

Grinuile (1595) in The Last Fight of the Revenge, ed.
Edmund Goldsmid (Edinburgh, 1886), II, 96: "Bassan... /
Swore the brave Knight nor ship he would not lose, /
Should all the world in a petition come."

256. did faine) Doubtless a bitter pun--"were glad" and "did
feign." Cf. unfainedly, 1. 263 below.

290. The...marble) Cf. Markham's Devoreux (1597), stanza 42:
"the marble-skye."

293. My...seale to) "My blood and oath shall lend authority
to all my words."

S.D. Enter Antipater) Antipater's exit prior to this entrance
is not indicated in the Quarto (see where he speaks last
at ll. 281ff.). Probably he merely goes to the door and
ushers in Pheroas and Achitophel.

416f. To...eternally) Cf. Richard II, V.iii.30 and 106:
"For ever may my knees grow to the earth"; and (106):
"Our knees shall kneel till to the ground they grow."

421f. The...sucke) Cf. Markham's A Health to...Serving-Men
(1598), sig. G3v: "Did he [Judas] not...goe foorth...
cursing...the wombe that bore him, and the pappes that
gave him sucke...?"

565-567. if...death) Cf. the Herod of York XIX, 125f.: "Thou
lyes! false traytoure strange, / Loke neuere þou negh
me nere."

II.i.

582.  center) of the earth.

590f.  The...t'imprison Oedipus) In Sophocles' Oedipus at
       Colonus, 11. 427-430, Oedipus states that his sons,
       Eteocles and Polyneices, consented to his banishment
       from Thebes; but there is no mention of his having been
       imprisoned.

Dumb shew.

       Cf. the following passage from Sallust's The two most
       worthy and notable histories, the Conspiracie of
       Cateline and the Warre which Jugurth maintained, trans.
       Thomas Heywood (1608-09; STC 21625), chap. II of the
       Warre: "[After the death of Micipsa, King of Numidia,
       his sons Jugurth, Adherbal, and Hiempsal] appointed a
       time of meeting, ther to take order for their further
       affaires.  Where Hiempsal (the youngest of the three,
       but by Nature the proudest) now, as before time, scorn-
       ing the base discent of Jugurth, by his mother
       [a concubine, Jugurth being a bastard], tooke place upon
       the right hand of Adherbal, that Jugurth might not sit in
       the midst; which amongst the Numidians is accounted the
       most Honourable place.  Neither could he by his Brothers
       earnest importunity, without apparant discontent, be per-
       swaded to remove on the other hand."  Shortly afterwards,
       Jugurth sent murderers to dispatch both brothers.

611.  descant) melodious accompaniment in counterpoint to a

II.i.

> plainsong. The musical terminology is complex in this
> passage. In the following line the meane is the middle
> part of the harmony; but in another sense it is the moder-
> ation, which is "excluded quite" since seven murders are
> being planned. Three lines later (615) diapason is the
> term for the consonance of the four voices, separated by
> intervals of an octave, sung together. In the same line
> the unison is probably not the agreement of the sounds,
> but the note taken as the starting-point from which the
> intervals are reckoned.

617. two brethren) Not clear. Pheroas is one brother who is
     still alive, but Joseph, Herod's brother-in-law, is
     already dead.

619. puny) novice or inferior, perhaps with the suggestion
     also of junior judge (puisne) in regard to understanding
     the "documents" or scrolls given by Jugurth and others.

622. The...cõmon) Cf. Markham's The first part of...the
     English Arcadia (1607; STC 17351), p. 63: "like an
     infant curtezan, who trembling at the first touch of
     sinne, growes by vse impudent in sinne..."

623. And...way?) Cf. Seneca, Agamemnon, 1. 150: "Res est
     profecto stulta nequitiae modus"--"Surely 'tis folly to
     stop midway in sin" (Miller, II, 14-15). Cf. also Macbeth,
     III.iv.136ff.: "I am in blood / Stepp'd in so far that,

II.i.

should I wade no more, / Returning were as tedious as

go o'er..."

654.    behinde) to come.

III.i.

20.    whipping on statute-lace) Statute-lace was ornamental

lace so-named because its width was fixed by statute.  The

pun involved may be threefold:  the beadle could be whip-

ping on (putting on quickly) a lace-trimmed coat; or

whipping (sewing with a whip-stitch) the lace on his coat;

or--as is obviously intended--punishing with a whip a bawd

or harlot (clothed in statute-lace) tied to a cart's tail

(see ll. 21-23 following).

70.    Treasure...tongue) Cf. Markham and Machin's The Dumb

Knight (1608) in Dodsley's Old English Plays (London,

1875), X, 192:  "this dumb god [gold] gives tongue to

all men."

74.    shadowes) The "slaves" (l. 73) being the princes, Antipater

seems here to be punning.  They will run to hell because of

false appearances (shadows), the letters and lies forged

against them; or they will run to hell to become phantoms

(shadows).

76.    tickle) precarious.

81.    free) noble and generous.

97.    Amorite) The Amorites were a wicked nation in the Bible

(see Genesis xiv.7 and passim), but the word is used here

III.i.

to suggest "lover." Markham used <u>Amorite</u> in the latter
sense elsewhere. See <u>Devoreux</u> (1597), stanza 39: "O
Fortune, thou great Amorite of Kings"; and <u>Rodomonths</u>
<u>Infernall</u> (1607), stanza 118: "Led by yong thoughts
(inamorites to will)..."

101. felters) tangles. Cf. Markham's <u>English</u> <u>Housewife</u> (1615),
II.v.: "If you find any hard knot or other felter in
the Wooll"--this quoted in the <u>OED</u>.

102. equipage) display or array.

131. balls) soap-balls.

139. Cry hem) clear the throat by coughing.

146. numbers) Humorous confusion of <u>numbers</u> as verses of
poetry.

198. forsworne) Ironically apropos error for <u>sworn</u>.

232. casting mines up) involved in crafty undermining of
their opposition (as in military use); or digging up
strange, hidden matters.

252. renowne) make famous.

286-289. for...it) Markham came close to this phrasing in other
places. Cf. <u>Devoreux</u> (1597), stanza 231: "Come, and ile
carry thee where Time hath set / His [Devoreux's] Tropheys
vp, to last when all things end"; and <u>Rodomonths</u> <u>Infer-</u>
<u>nall</u>, (1607), stanza 63: "(Trophees that time nor ruine
should down raze)." Cf. also the threat that the
Towneley Herod makes, after hearing that his soldiers

III.i.

have slain 144,000 children: "Thus shall I tech knauys /
ensampyll to take....youre nekkys shall I shak / In
sonder...many oone shall / Apon youre bodys wonder"
(XVI, 496-504).

315f.  which...grafting) Apparently the antecedent of which is
branch (Antipater), held in low repute because he was
improperly "grafted," i.e., born a bastard.

366.  paunce) pansy.

390.  polipode of the oake) "This polypody, it is a fern that
groweth upon oaks....It hath virtue of dissolving, of
drawing and of purging phlegm, and especially melan-
choly..."--An Herbal (1525), ed. Sanford V. Larkey, M.D.,
and Thomas Pyles (New York, 1941), pp. 63f.

391.  vervine) vervain, sometimes called "holy herb," hence
(perhaps) "chast"; said, in the old herbals, to cure
many ills.

391.  eringo) sea-holly root, supposedly "good for...people
that haue no delight or appetite to venery"--The Herball
or generall historie of Plantes by John Gerarde (London,
1597), p. 1000.

IV.i.

122f.  adde...water) Cf. Markham's Marie Magdalens Lamentations

IV.i.

(1601; STC 17569), Second Lamentation, stanza 12:

"my teares... / Are rather oile than water to my flame."

158. Mount...ground) Cf. Richard II, V.v.112f.: "Mount, mount,
my soul! thy seat is up on high; / Whilst my gross flesh
sinks downward, here to die."

IV.ii.

30. the fishes dance) Cf. Markham's The Newe Metamorphosis
in J. H. H. Lyon's A Study of The Newe Metamorphosis
(New York, 1919), p. 89: "There sportive fishes...dance
in brightest streames..."

31. Cedron) Sometimes spelled Kidron, a river near Jerusalem.
Cf. John xviii.1 and II Samuel xv.23.

38. Of...Arabia) Cf. Markham's The Poem of Poems (1596;
STC 17386), sig. B3v: "purest gold...from out the'Arabian
mine." See also Herod and Antipater, V.i.10.

40. Ophyr) Job xxii.24: A place from which fine gold was
obtained.

48f. that...equal'd) Cf. Markham's The Poem of Poems, Ecloga
Tertia: "King Salomon...for himselfe a stately pallace
fram'd...Such as no after age shall euer knowe."

92. mother) mother-in-law, Alexandra.

270. Carry...cunningly) Cf. the strategy of the medieval
Herod, when sending his herald to bring the Magi before
him: "But I warne the that thy wordis be milde, / For
there must thow hede and crafte weylde / How to for-do

IV.ii.

his [Christ's] power" (Coventry *Pageant of the Shearmen and Taylors*, 11. 619-621).

286. No...Destinie) Cf. Markham's *The Tragedie of Sir Richard Grinuile* (1595) in *The Last Fight of the Revenge*, ed. Edmund Goldsmid (Edinburgh, 1886), II, 20: "But men, are men, in ignorance of Fate, / To alter chaunce, exceedeth humaine state."

V.i.

29-31. Has...made) Cf. *Richard III*, I.i.16, 19-21: "I, that am rudely stamp'd,... / Cheated of feature by dissembling nature, / Deform'd, unfinish'd, sent before my time / Into this breathing world, scarce half made up..."

40. wood-cracks) wood-crackers, nuthatches.

48. freer in guift) nobler in natural endowment.

96f. Have...first) Cf. *Richard II*, III.ii.131: "Snakes, in my heart-blood warm'd, that sting my heart!"

150. mother) mother-in-law. For "brothers" and "sisters" in this line, see note 69 in the Appendix Concerning Sources (1. 182 below).

200. A...stone) Cf. Markham and Machin's *The Dumb Knight* (1608) in *Dodsley's Old English Plays* (London, 1875), X, 123f., where a husband's eyes are said to be "able to pierce through a / millstone."

204. us two) Herod and Antipater.

V.ii.

10. serio joco) serious play.

79. ginger-bread) fig.: "pretended prudence."

85f. All...creation) Cf. Richard II, I.iii.214f.: "Four
lagging winters and four wanton springs / End in a word:
such is the breath of kings."

186. Why...conscience) Cf. Richard's attitude in Richard III,
V.iii.308f.: "Let not our babbling dreams affright our
souls, / For conscience is a word that cowards use."

263. Mountaines...Jupiter) A second allusion (see I.iii.352
above) to the attack of the giants against heaven.  In the
war the giants threw great rocks up at Zeus (Jupiter) from
the mountain tops where they launched their revolt.

296. Greatnesse...cradle) Cf. Markham's Honour in his Perfection
1624; STC 17361), p. 18: "his cradle did point him out a
Souldier."

318. that) the body of Antipater.

320. admire) wonder at.

The Epilogue.

8. A...told) Cf. Sampson's The Vow Breaker (1636), Prologue,
l. 1f.: "Truth saies the Author, this Time will be bold /
To tell a Story, truer ne're was told..."  The Renaissance
historiographers, especially the Jacobeans, "had come to
place a premium upon truth as an end in itself" (Ribner,
English History Play, p. 299).  Thomas Heywood, in the
preface to his translation of Sallust (1608-09), emphasized

The Epilogue.

this point: "Historie ought to be nothing but a representation of truth, and as it were a Map of mens actions,
sette forth in the publicke view of all commers to bee
examined" (Sallust, The Conspiracy of Catiline and The
War of Jugurtha, trans. Thomas Heywood, with an introduction by Charles Whibley--New York, 1924--p. 16. In this
preface Heywood was actually translating Chapter IV of
Jean Bodin's Methodus ad facilem historiarum cognitionem
of 1566). Before Heywood, Thomas Blundeville expressed
the same view in The True Order and Methode of Wryting
and Reading Hystories (1574): Historiographers should
"tell things as they were done with out...swarving one
iote from the truth" (Quoted by Leonard F. Dean, "Tudor
Theories of History Writing," University of Michigan
Contributions in Modern Philology, No. 1--April, 1947--
p. 5).

## AN APPENDIX CONCERNING SOURCES

The intent of this appendix is to compare three historical accounts which may have served as sources for the play. These are Flavius Josephus's The Warres of the Iewes and The Antiquities of the Iewes, translated from Latin and French into English by Thomas Lodge in 1602 (STC 14809), and Joseph ben Gorion's A Compendious History of the Iewes Commune Weale, translated purportedly from Hebrew into English by Peter Morwyng in 1558 (STC 14795). Of these the last seems certainly to have been the playwrights' main reference.

The indebtedness to Morwyng was first noticed by A. M. Silbermann in his Untersuchungen über die Quellen des Dramas, The True Tragedy of Herod and Antipater (Wittenberg, 1922). Here he compares the account given by the play to the accounts of Josephus and The Commune Weale, and also to those of Ben Daûd, Münster, and Lepusculus (See Introduction, pp. viii-ix). Most of the play's material is shown to agree with The Commune Weale, but occasionally (p. 52 and p. 86) Silbermann admits that the playwrights must have glanced at one of the other accounts.

What Silbermann fails to suggest, however, is the possibility that Lodge's translations were used. Instead, he cites only the Latin texts of Josephus. Considering that Lodge's translations went through three printings prior to 1622, when the play appeared, it seems possible that Markham and Sampson knew these works. For this reason in the following notes Lodge's Josephus is cited.

The appendix hopefully will serve as more than a simple restatement of Silbermann's work. In fact I have compiled it independently of the _Untersuchungen_, the latter study coming into my hands only after I had first drafted these notes. I was gratified, though not surprised, to find that Silbermann and I concurred on many observations. I have accordingly indicated this agreement in many of the notes. Also Silbermann gave me a clearer perception in some cases, and especially in the distinctions of note 15.

In many cases, however, I have gone further than Silbermann by making comparisons and delineations which he did not mention. Yet nothing I have discovered greatly alters the truth of Silbermann's work, but instead in the main reinforces it.

Finally, since Morwyng ascribed _The Commune Weale_ to Ben Gorion, I have used Ben Gorion's name in referring to it. For the real derivation of this work, however, see the Introduction (pp. viii-ix). For convenience also I have spelled the characters' names as they appear in the play, since the spellings often vary in the histories.

[1]Antigonus (1. 19) was Marriam's uncle, the brother of her father Alexander (1. 22). He was beheaded by Anthony for trying to seize control of Jerusalem at the time the Roman senate proclaimed Herod king of the Jews. In _The_ _Antiq_. Herod bribed Anthony to kill Antigonus (_Antiq_., XIIII:XXVIII,381; _Warres_, I:XIII,583). However, Ben Gorion says that it was Cassius who slew Antigonus for Herod (fol. xxxix b),

as Alexandra states in I.iii.167. Silbermann notes this difference
(p. 40). See below, note 8.

Hircanus (l. 22), Alexandra's father, was both king and High
Priest of the Jews before Herod came to power. In Ben Gorion and in
The Antiq., Herod executed him for plotting to flee to Arabia (Ben
Gorion, fol. xlii a; and Antiq., XV:IX,394). See below, I.iii.164f.
The escape to Arabia is not mentioned in The Warres (I:XVII,589).

Alexander (l. 22) was husband of Alexandra and nephew of
Hircanus. He was beheaded by Scipio at Pompey's command, not Herod's,
for trying to seize control of Jerusalem when Hircanus was king
(Warres, I:VII,570; and Antiq., XIIII:XIII,359). Ben Gorion does not
relate his death, but says that Alexandra blamed Herod for it (fol.
xlv a--see note 17 below). Also in The Antiq. Marriam accused Herod
of killing Alexander (XV:XI,398). Cf. I.iii.169.

[2]Historically, Antipater was a bastard in a figurative sense
only. His mother was a woman Herod married before becoming king.
Josephus gives her name as Doris (Warres, I:X,574; Antiq., XIIII:XXI,
368), though she is called Rostios in the text of Ben Gorion and Dosis
in the marginalia (fol. lii b and lx b). In none of the accounts,
nevertheless, was Antipater at court when Marriam was accused and executed. He was brought to court when discord arose between Herod and
his two sons by Marriam (Warres, I:XVII,590; Antiq., XVI:VI,416;
and Ben Gorion, fol. liii a).

[3]The secret correspondence between Alexandra and Cleopatra is mentioned in The Antiq. (XV:III,385) and in Ben Gorion (fol. xliii b). Cleopatra's reply shows no verbal indebtedness to either account. Alexandra appears only once in The Warres, where a brief reference is made to her as Marriam's mother (I:XI,576). She is not named, and for all purposes she has no rôle in the narrative.

[4]In the accounts of Josephus and Ben Gorion the two sons of Marriam play no part in the history until after her death. They do not appear at her trial.

[5]The attempted escape in the trunks is recorded in The Antiq.-- where the trunks are actually coffins--(XV:III,385) and in Ben Gorion (fol. xliii b), but not in The Warres. In both accounts Herod was told beforehand of the device and caught Alexandra and her son in the very act. In Josephus, Herod forgave them because he feared Cleopatra's hatred of him, but "vnder the colour of a high and magnanimous spirit, he made shewe to pardon her of his meere clemencie" (XV:III,385). In Ben Gorion, after a sharp exchange of words, Herod simply "dissembled the matter & shewed no great displeasure" (fol. xliiii a).

[6]Alexandra's historical queenship was short-lived, and in fact she is never called queen in any of the three accounts. Josephus does state that Alexander, her husband, took "possession of the kingdome" (Antiq., XIIII:XI,357); and Ben Gorion says that the Israelites resorted unto Alexander and "made him kinge in Hircanus place"

(fol. xxxii a).  But in both histories he was quickly overpowered by the Romans.  See also Warres, I:VI,568.

[7]For Hircanus, see note 1 above.

[8]Antigonus (1. 168):  Alexandra seems here to confuse her parentage, since in I.i.21f. above she has already identified Hircanus, and not Antigonus, as her father.  For the reference to Cassius (1. 167), see note 1 above.

[9]"Holines / Vpon my right hand" may have been suggested by Ben Gorion on the page following the affair of the coffins.  Here, at a feast given by Herod, "Aristobulus the hie priest, he set vpō his righthand" (fol. xliiii b).

[10]Historically, Herod aided Anthony because of their friendship and the many favors Anthony had done for him (Warres, I:XV,585; Antiq., XV:X,395; and Ben Gorion, fol. xlvi a).

[11]Ben Gorion states that at Rhodes Herod "hauinge his croune vpon his head; he toke it of, & fel down prostrate vppon the ground at Octauians feete" (fol. xlvi b).  Josephus records that Herod merely removed his crown (Warres, I:XV,585; and Antiq., XV:X,395).

[12]In Ben Gorion Herod left Joseph his uncle in charge of his "houshold" while he was at Rhodes (fol. xlvi a).  In The Antiq. he gave Pheroas charge of the kingdom, but told Joseph his treasurer to watch over Marriam and her mother (XV:IX,395).  For the two different

Josephs, see note 15 below.  See this note also for the account in
The Warres.

$^{13}$No swimming match, as such, was related in any of the histories
Yet in Ben Gorion when Aristobulus requested permission to swim, Herod
denied him at first (11. 281f.).  Silbermann notes this (p. 42).  To his
servants, however, "the king had geuen secret cõmaundemente, that they
shoulde desire Aristobulus to go and bathe with them in Iordane, and
then to drown him" (fol. xliiii b).  In The Antiq. Herod prompted the
High Priest to swim, where those appointed drowned him (XV:III,386).
In The Warres Herod sent him to Jericho where certain "Galatheans"
drowned him at the king's command (I:XVII,589).  The drowning did not
occur while Herod was at Rhodes in either Josephus or Ben Gorion.
(Aristobulus was only 18 years old when he died--Antiq., XV:III,386).

$^{14}$The drowning occurred at night (or evening) in Josephus
(Warres, I:XVII,589; and Antiq., XV:III,386) and in Ben Gorion (fol.
xlv a).

$^{15}$Concerning this command the histories differ on two main
points.  The first is the occasion on which Herod left the command;
the second is the identity of the man with whom he left it.  The
different accounts are as follows.

In Ben Gorion, as in the play, Herod went before Augustus
at Rhodes and he left the command with Joseph his uncle, who was
Salumith's husband.

In The Warres Herod went not before Augustus, but instead before Anthony.  He left the command again with Joseph his uncle.  (The

motive for this trip is not stated clearly:  presumably Herod went to answer for the death of Aristobulus, as he did in The Antiq.)

In The Antiq. Herod left the command on two separate occasions-- once before going to Anthony and once again before going to Augustus. In the first case he went to account for Aristobulus, and he left the command with Joseph his uncle.  In the second case he went to account for his aid to Anthony, and this time he left the command with Joseph his treasurer (not uncle) and also with a man named Sohemus.  Further- more, he commanded these two to kill both Marriam and her mother should he fail to return.

Thus, as Silbermann observes (p. 45), only in Ben Gorion do the details of this episode match those of the play--the trip to Rhodes before Augustus, the command revealed by Joseph, Salumith's husband, and the command over Marriam alone.  (Cf. Ben Gorion, fol. xlvi a; Warres, I:XVII,589; and Antiq., XV:IIII,387 and XV:IX,395).

[16]Herod's secret commands were overheard in none of the histories.

[17]In The Antiq. although Alexandra knew that her son was mur- dered, she hid her knowledge in hopes of later taking revenge on Herod (XV:III,386).  In Ben Gorion, however, "Alexandra his mother in law letted not to tell it him to his face, that he was y[e] murtherer of her husband, and her father, & now last of al her sonne" (fol. xlv a).  She does not appear at this point in The Warres. Silbermann observes her reaction in Ben Gorion (p. 49).  Cf. below, II.i.203f.

[18] In _The Warres_ Joseph's motive for revealing the command was only to demonstrate Herod's love for Marriam (I:XVII,589). This was also the reason in _The Antiq._ (XV:IIII,387), though Sohemus revealed the second command (see note 15 above) to gain political favor with the queen (XV:XI,397). Ben Gorion does not give Joseph's motive (fol. xlvii _b_).

[19] The sexual jealousy of Salumith towards Marriam and Joseph seems original in the play. In _The Warres_ she hated Marriam for upbraiding her (I:XVII,589). In _The Antiq._ she hated Marriam for scorning her "obscure birth" (XV:IIII,388). Yet in both these accounts Salumith falsely accused Marriam of adultery with Joseph, which Herod suspected when his secret command was revealed (_Warres_, I:XVII,590; and _Antiq._, XV:IIII,388). See II.i.159f. below. Ben Gorion likewise states that Marriam reproached Salumith for her "vnholy" and "base" birth (fol. xlv _b_) and that Salumith calumniated the queen regarding Joseph (fol. xlviii _a_).

[20] Herod's defense of himself before Augustus follows Ben Gorion's account more closely than it does either of Josephus's. Here Herod stated, in part: "I cõfesse therfore y$^t$ in his warres against your maiesty, I aided him..." (Cf. 1. 21f.) "And it is true, y$^t$ your maiesty sẽce the time you made me king, haue herd of mine affaires y$^t$ haue happened vnto me, but neuer succoured me. This _M. Antonius_ did not so." (Cf. 1. 36f.) And possibly: "When he [Anthony] was falling, I bolsterd him vp." (Cf. 1. 41f.) (All fol. xlvi _b_). Cf.

Warres (I:XV,585f.) and Antiq. (XV:X,395f.).  Silbermann notes these
similarities (p. 47).

[21]Anthony sent military aid to Herod against Antigonus (note 1
above) and his Jewish and Parthian supporters (Warres, I:XII,580;
Antiq., XIIII:XXVII,375; and Ben Gorion, fol. xxxviii a & b).

[22]In all three histories Augustus pardoned Herod immediately
after the defense speech (Warres, I:XV,586; Antiq., XV:X,396; and
Ben Gorion, fol. xlvii a, but actually misnumbered fol. lxvii a).
In The Warres he told Herod:  "Liue in safetie....endeuour thy
selfe to continue faithfull.." (Cf. 11. 109f.)

[23]Ben Gorion notes the "perpetual hatred betwene Alexandra &
Marimi, and Kiparim the mother of Herode, & Salumith his sister
that came of base & seruile blud.  For Marimi cast in their teethe
to their faces, that they wer not of the sede of Israel:  but vnholy
& of base birth" (fol. xlv b).  Marriam likewise slandered Herod's
mother in The Antiq. (XV:XI,398).  See also note 19 above.

[24]The term "Greeke" has no basis in Josephus.  Herod and
Salumith's father was an Idumean, and their mother an Arabian
(Warres; I:V,565 and I:VI,569; Antiq., XIIII:II,350 and XIIII:XII,
359).  In Ben Gorion the father was learned "in the knowledge of
the Greke."  But "His ofspringe was not out of the children of
Israell, but of those Romaines which chaūced to be vanquished, &
became subiect vnder the dominion of the Israelits, being but
straūgers, & of no noble house in Israel" (fol. xxvii a).  Kiparim's
race is not specified.  See also 1. 120 below.

[25]"him that wore the Crowne" is a mysterious allusion.
Alexandra had only one son, Aristobulus, as is stated in The Antiq.
(XV:II,384). This is also true in The Warres and in Ben Gorion.

[26]Kiparim was herself a "base Edomite." (See note 24 above,
Idumea being another name for Edom.) Alexandra was descended from
the royal Jewish line of Hasmonaeans that derived from Asmonaeus,
an early priest of Jerusalem (Antiq., XII:VIII,304; Warres, I:I,
559; and Ben Gorion, fol. iiii b).

[27]In The Warres Aristobulus was drowned in a "lake" in Jericho
(I:XVII,589); in The Antiq. in the "fishpooles" there (XV:III,386);
and in Ben Gorion in the "Iordane" (fol. xliiii b). Rigall is
unidentified.

[28]Regarding Salumith's slander of Marriam, see note 19 above.
Herod's refusal to believe his sister may stem from Ben Gorion:
"Herode (saye what she could) gaue no credite to her wordes, know-
ing that she enuied Marimi" (fol. xlviii a). This detail does not
occur in Josephus.

[29]Herod displayed sorrow for Aristobulus in Ben Gorion and
The Antiq. (fol. xlv a; and XV:III,386); and both accounts suggest
that he may have truly repented. Mention of the funeral (1. 213)
occurs only in The Antiq. The Warres tells only of the drowning
(I:XVII,589).

[30]Marriam confronted Herod with his command to Joseph in all
three of the histories, though not with the command to Sohemus in

the second incident in The Antiq. (Warres, I:XVII,589; Antiq., XV:IIII,388 and XV:XI,398; and Ben Gorion, fol. xlviii a).

[31]The story of the poisoned love potion is told against Marriam in The Antiq. and in Ben Gorion, but not in The Warres. In The Antiq., however, it occurs as part of the Sohemus story when the secret command was betrayed the second time. In this account the cupbearer is not identified, though he was sent by Salumith to accuse Marriam (XV:XI,398). In Ben Gorion's account the details are even less precise: Salumith hired "false accusars and forgers of lies, to witnes that Marimi woulde haue poysoned the kinge" (fol. xlviii b); but here the poison is not called a love potion.

[32]The historical figure represented by Achitophel did not appear at Marriam's trial in either The Antiq. or Ben Gorion. (In The Warres the poison plot is lacking.) See below, note 52.

[33]This cowardly accusation of Marriam by her mother is recorded in The Antiq. and in Ben Gorion (XV:XI,399; and fol. xlviii b), though the present speeches follow neither account. In Ben Gorion Alexandra hoped by her action to survive long enough to poison Herod (fol. xlix a). She was not at the trial in The Warres.

[34]In The Warres and in Ben Gorion (see note 15 above) Herod slew his uncle Joseph and Marriam because he suspected them of adultery (I:XVII,590; and fol. xlix a & b). In The Antiq. he spared Marriam after the first command was revealed, but he killed his uncle

(XV:IIII,388). Later, however, when Sohemus revealed the second command, Herod put him and Marriam to death, but spared Joseph the treasurer (XV:XI,398).

[35]The mode of Marriam's death--beheading--and the place of execution--the market place--are specified only in Ben Gorion (fol. xlviii b). Cf. Antiq., XV:XI,398; and Warres, I:XVII,590.

[36]The words of the princes echo those of Alexander in Ben Gorion: "How can I forget the mooste chaste wombe that bare me, whiche was of the holye stocke?" (fol. liii b). Cf. ll. 420f. and l. 424. Silbermann notes this indebtedness (p. 51). But in the history Alexander asked this question before Augustus in Rome. See note 40 below.

[37]In The Antiq. Herod was reluctant to have Marriam killed, even though he had condemned her. Salumith urged her death, "least some sedition should be raised amongst the people, if he should keepe her aliue" (XV:XI,398). These details are missing in the other accounts.

[38]In both accounts by Josephus Herod pretended that Marriam was still alive. In The Warres he talked to her (I:XVII,590); and in The Antiq. he had his ministers call for her (XV:XI,399). In Ben Gorion he fell sick after her death but engaged in no fantasy (fol. xlix b).

[39]Pheroas was banished in both The Warres and The Antiq. because his wife angered Herod, not because of anything he said

about Marriam (<u>Warres</u>, I:XIX,599; and <u>Antiq</u>., XVII:V,440). In Ben Gorion he was banished because of a dangerous league he formed with Antipater (fol. lviii <u>b</u>).

[40]The historical sons of Marriam never raised arms against Herod, though they did come to great discord with him after her death. In <u>The Warres</u> Herod accused Alexander, before Augustus in Rome, of trying to poison him (I:XVII,590). Likewise in <u>The Antiq</u>. he accused both sons of this, and Antipater was also present (XVI: VII,417). In both cases Augustus reconciled them. In Ben Gorion Alexander alone was arraigned (fol. liii <u>a</u>). Following the incident, in <u>The Warres</u> and in Ben Gorion Herod divided the kingdom between his three sons (I:XVII,591; and fol. liiii <u>a</u>). In <u>The Antiq</u>. he named Antipater first in the order of succession (XVI: VIII,420). Cf. 11. 649f.

[41]The workmen were suborned against the princes in none of the histories.

[42]The dimensions given here for each stone do not agree with those given in either <u>The Antiq</u>. (XV:XIIII,409) or Ben Gorion (fol. li <u>a</u>). None are given in <u>The Warres</u>. But see note 54 below.

[43]Similar counterfeit letters were produced against the princes in all three histories, and Antipater seemed to be the author in each case (<u>Warres</u>, I:XVII,596; <u>Antiq</u>., XVI:XVI,431; and Ben Gorion, fol. lvii <u>a</u>). Yet the name <u>Chrysander</u> appears in none of the accounts. Silbermann calls it an invention (p. 52).

[44] In _The Warres_ Herod fancied he saw Alexander coming after him with a sword (I:XVII,593); and in _The Antiq_. he thought he saw both sons (XVI:XI,427). Ben Gorion tells how Antipater "hired fals witnesses to say they saw _Alexander_ the kinges sonne vppon a certaine night with his sword drawn before the kinges palaice, mindinge to murther _Antipater_" (fol. lv _a_). Silbermann observes that the nighttime and the king's palace are details only in Ben Gorion (p. 53).

[45] Antipater gave like warning to Salumith in Ben Gorion: "doest thou not consider how the sonnes of _Marimi_ knowe y$^t$ their mother was put to death by thy counsel. Therfore if they maye bringe to passe to make the king away: they wil hew thee to peces" (fol. liiii _b_).

[46] The barber's love for Salumith is original in the play. See further, note 48 below.

[47] Antipater subtly apologized for the princes in both accounts by Josephus--"that making a shew of good will vnto them he might secretly oppresse them the sooner" (_Antiq_., XVI:XI,423);--and "nothing made so much credit be giuẽ to these calumniations, as that _Antipater_ colorably excused his brother" (_Warres_, I:XVII,591).

[48] In _The Warres_ and _The Antiq_. the barber Tryphon told Herod that Tyro, an agent for Alexander, had urged him to cut Herod's throat. For this, Tryphon was stoned to death. Antipater was not implicated (_Warres_, I:XVII,597; and _Antiq_., XVI:XVII,435). Ben Gorion says that Antipater was responsible for the barber's false

witness that Alexander had hired him to kill Herod.  Here the barber
met an unspecified execution, and his name also was not given (fol.
lvii <u>a</u> & <u>b</u>).  Silbermann notes the omission of the name (p. 52).

[49]After the barber incident, Ben Gorion quotes Herod as saying:
"who soeuer bringes me ani such tales hereafter of any bodi, / he
shall suffer death for it" (fol. lvii <u>a</u> & <u>b</u>).  Josephus does not
mention this.

[50]In Josephus's accounts Herod sent his sons to Sebaste and
had them strangled there (<u>Warres</u>, I:XVII,597; and <u>Antiq.</u>, XVI:XVII,
435).  In Ben Gorion they were "hanged vpon gallowes" (fol. lvii <u>b</u>),
presumably in Herod's sight.

[51]In the histories Herod sent Antipater to Augustus as his
successor (<u>Warres</u>, I:XVIII,599; <u>Antiq.</u>, XVII:IIII,440; and Ben Gorion,
fol. lix <u>a</u>).

[52]Ben Gorion states that in Egypt Antipater met a merchant
"hauinge a Vyall in his hande close couered, which cried saying:
who wil bie a thing at a great price before he see it, or know what
it is?  <u>Antipater</u> meruailed at his words, and asked him what was
in his Vyal.  But the seller tolde him not what it was, before he
hadde bought it and paide deare for it.  Then whispered he in his
eare, tellinge him that it was a strong poison, that would kil one
out of hand" (fol. lix <u>a</u>).  (Silbermann notes this similarity,
pp. 53-54.)  This merchant is not named.  In <u>The</u> <u>Warres</u> and <u>The</u>
<u>Antiq.</u> the poison was acquired in Egypt for Antipater by a friend

named Antiphilus (Achitophel?) (<u>Warres</u>, I:XIX,600; and <u>Antiq</u>., XVII: VI,441).

[53]In all three histories, before dying, Pheroas repented of his plots against Herod. But in Josephus he ordered the poison burned, whereas in Ben Gorion he ordered it spilled on the ground (<u>Warres</u>, I:XIX,601; <u>Antiq</u>., XVII:VI,442; and Ben Gorion, fol. lxi <u>b</u>).

[54]Though Josephus describes the temple extensively in <u>The Antiq</u>. (XV:XIIII,409-411) and to a lesser degree in <u>The Warres</u> (I: XVI,586), the present description unmistakably follows Ben Gorion: "So he pulled downe the house and repaired it again...in length a hundred cubites, in bredth lykewise a hundreth cubites, and in height a hundreth cubites, all of white marble....the foundacion was .xx. cubites within the grounde...The / breadth of euery stone was .xii. cubites, and the thicknes thereof .viii. cubites, euery stone was of like bignesse. The gates of the house he couered with fine gold and precious stoones finely sette therin: the thresholdes were of siluer & y$^e$ tops also. He made also a vine of gold a marveilous cunning pece of worcke, the armes therof or bigger braunches were glittering gold, the lesser braunches, slips, or latest shutes of gold, sumwhat red: & al aboue was yelow gold, wherupon hong clusters of cristal....In all the world was not the like to be seen....he made a court...whiche was paued with pure marble....He erected...pillers of white marble.... / and euerye piller was .xl. cubites hie....Toward the east the court conteined .D. ccxx. cubites...No man euer se the like building in all the world....he made also walkes and...galeries of such height: that

they y^t walked therin might easily se the waters running in the
broke <u>Cedron</u>....the king made a wal of siluer, of halfe a handful
thicke.  In the which was a dore of beaten golde, and vpon the gate
a sword of golde...There were certain poses grauen in the sworde, as
this.  <u>VVhat</u> <u>straunger</u> <u>so</u> <u>euer</u> <u>approcheth</u> <u>nie</u> <u>her</u>, <u>let</u> <u>him</u> <u>die</u> <u>for</u>
<u>it</u>" (fol. 1 <u>b</u> -1i <u>b</u>).  Silbermann calls this "irrefutable evidence"
that Morwyng was used (p. 56).

[55]The eunuch appears only in Ben Gorion.  After Pheroas died,
his wife and Antipater quarreled.  To betray her, Antipater sent a
eunuch to Herod with a story of the poison plot in which Pheroas
and his wife were alone responsible (fol. lix <u>b</u>).  In Josephus,
although Salumith spied on Antipater and Pheroas for Herod, she
seems not to have known about the poison (<u>Antiq</u>., XVII:III,439; and
<u>Warres</u>, I:XVIII,599).

[56]Pheroas's wife lept from the housetop in all three histories,
though she did not fall on the soldiers (1. 124).  In <u>The Antiq</u>. she
admitted having the poison before she lept (<u>Antiq</u>., XVII:VI,441;
<u>Warres</u>, I:XIX,600; and Ben Gorion, fol. lxi <u>a</u>).  Her name is given
in none of the accounts.

[57]In the three histories the fear of torture was enough to
make Pheroas's wife confess.  She was not racked (<u>Warres</u>, I:XIX,600;
<u>Antiq</u>., XVII:VI,441; and Ben Gorion, foL lxi <u>a</u>).

[58]Pheroas's wife betrayed Antipater to Herod in all three
histories (<u>Warres</u>, I:XIX,600; <u>Antiq</u>., XVII:VI,442; and Ben Gorion,
fol. lxi <u>a</u>).

[59]Josephus: "the most part of the poison I cast into the fire...& kept a little therof to my self" (Warres, I:XIX,601). Ben Gorion: "I did as he bad me, cast it out al saue a litle that I kepte in the glase botome" (fol. lxi b).

[60]In Ben Gorion, Alexandra was killed by Herod for trying to poison him, though her attempt was made some time before Antipater's (fol. xlix b). In The Antiq. she was slain by Herod for trying to take control of some of his strongholds (XV:XI,400). Silbermann notes this difference (p. 56). Alexandra's death is not mentioned in The Warres.

Also, in both accounts by Josephus Antiphilus was not killed, but his mother and brother were tortured (Warres, I:XIX,601; and Antiq. XVII:VI, 442). In Ben Gorion the death of the merchant who sold the poison is not mentioned.

[61]Salumith was not incriminated in this plot in any of the histories.

[62]In the histories Herod concealed from Antipater the fact that his treachery had been discovered (Warres, I:XX,601; Antiq., XVII:VII,422; and Ben Gorion, fol. lxi b).

[63]Ben Gorion alone states that Herod's physicians healed Pheroas's wife and that she recovered (fol. lxi b).

[64]In Ben Gorion and The Warres Antipater was avoided by all men when he came home (fol. lxii b; and I:XX,602). In The Antiq. he was "bitterly cursed" (XVII:VII,443).

[65]In each of the histories some of Antipater's friends urged him to return home from Rome immediately so as not to give further weight to the suspicions already against him (Warres, I:XX,602; Antiq., XVII:VII,443; and Ben Gorion, fol. lxii a).

[66]In The Antiq. Herod wept at the beginning of the trial because of his own misfortunes, not Antipater's. Yet, following his son's defense speech, Herod "made it appeare, that he seemed in some sort to be altered in his opinion: notwithstanding he enduoured [sic] to conceale the same" (XVII:VII,444). And in none of the accounts did he once begin to pardon Antipater.

In Josephus, Nicholaus Damascene accused Antipater at the trial (Warres, I:XX,604; and Antiq., XVII:VII,444). In Ben Gorion the name given is "Niraleus the kings secretary" (fol. lxiii a). Silbermann notes this difference (p. 60).

[67]Marriam's name did not arise at the trial in either account by Josephus. But Ben Gorion tells how at one point "with a loude voice the king burst out and bewailed his wife Marimi, whõ he put to death without a cause" (fol. lxiii a). Herod did not blame Antipater for her death, however.

[68]Ben Gorion: "Woe may he bee, that hathe none left to succede him" (fol. lxiii b). Herod said this just before he tried to stab himself.

[69]Herod had three brothers but only one sister (Antiq. XIIII: XII,359; Warres, I:VI,569; and Ben Gorion, fol. xxvii a). Two of his brothers were killed in the wars fought against Antigonus (note

1 above--Antiq., XIIII:XXV,373 and XIIII:XXVII,378; Warres, I:XI, 576 and I:XIII,580; and Ben Gorion, fol. xxxvii b and xxxviii b).

[70]Archelaus and Antipas were historically Herod's children, not his grandchildren (Warres, I:XVIII,598; Antiq., XVII:I,437; and Ben Gorion, fol. lxv a and lxvii a). They were born of Herod's wife Malthace, a Samaritan (Warres, I:XVIII,598). (He had ten wives in all.)

[71]Herod tried to stab himself in all three histories, but was prevented by those around him (Warres, I:XXI,606; Antiq., XVII:IX, 450; and Ben Gorion, fol. lxiiii a). In Josephus he despaired because of old age and sickness. In Ben Gorion, in addition to these motives, he remembered "Marimi, and his two sonnes" just before the attempt.

[72]In all three accounts the lament raised over Herod's attempted suicide reached Antipater in jail, causing him to think the king dead (Warres, I:XXI,606; Antiq., XVII:IX,450; and Ben Gorion, fol. lxiiii a).

[73]The name Chasmonani for the royal family occurs only in Ben Gorion (fol. liiii b), as Silbermann notes (p. 61). The name in Josephus is Asmoneans (Antiq., XIIII:XXVIII,381). Neither name appears in The Warres.

[74]Augustus did not come to Jerusalem for the execution of Antipater in any of the three histories. In Josephus's accounts he

condoned the death by letter from Rome (<u>Warres</u>, I:XXI,605; and

<u>Antiq</u>., XVII:IX,450). Ben Gorion has nothing to say about this.

[75] In Ben Gorion, Antipater tried to bribe the jailer, but

this man feared that Herod might still be alive (Cf. 1. 73). He

therefore went to Herod and told him that Antipater was "verie

glad" to hear of his father's death (fol. lxiiii <u>b</u>). The king then

"commaũded the kepar to bring him forth to the market place: which

dooen, his head was smiten of" (fol. lxv <u>a</u>). In Josephus, as soon

as Herod heard about the bribe, he sent his guard to kill Antipater

(<u>Warres</u>, I:XXI,606; and <u>Antiq</u>., XVII:IX,450).

[76] In none of the histories was Antipater falsely hailed as king.

[77] Antipater never admitted his guilt in the histories, nor did

he incriminate Salumith. Furthermore, she did not die in prison. In

Josephus, Herod left gifts to her in his will (<u>Warres</u>, I:XX,604; and

<u>Antiq</u>., XVII:X,450). Ben Gorion does not account for her end.

[78] Actually, Herod survived Antipater five days (<u>Warres</u>, I:XXI,

606; <u>Antiq</u>., XVII:X,450; and Ben Gorion, fol. lxv <u>a</u>).

[79] In Josephus, though Herod named Archelaus his successor,

Augustus confirmed this son only as ethnarch of one half of the

kingdom (<u>Warres</u>, II:IIII,613; and <u>Antiq</u>., XVII:XIII,459). In Ben

Gorion Augustus "cõfirmed & assured the kingdom to Archelaus" (fol.

lxvi <u>b</u>).

BIBLIOGRAPHY

Adams, J. Q., Jr. "Every Woman in her Humor and The Dumb Knight," Modern Philology, X (1913), 413-432.

Ben Gorion, Joseph. A Compendious History of the Iewes Commune Weale, trans. Peter Morwyng. London, 1558.

Bentley, G. E. The Jacobean and Caroline Stage. 5 vols. Oxford, 1941-56.

Chambers, Sir E. K. The Medieval Stage. 2 vols. Oxford, 1903.

Corrections and Additions to The Dictionary of National Biography. Boston, 1966. (Prepared by The Institute of Historical Research, London.)

Craig, Hardin, ed. Two Coventry Corpus Christi Plays. London, 1902.

Davies, Godfrey. The Early Stuarts 1603-1660. Oxford, 1937.

Dean, Leonard F. "Tudor Theories of History Writing," University of Michigan Contributions in Modern Philology, No. 1 (April, 1947).

Dunstan, A. C. Examination of Two English Dramas: 'The Tragedy of Mariam' by Elizabeth Carew; and 'The True Tragedy of Herod and Antipater, with the Death of Faire Marriam' by Gervase Markham and William Sampson. Königsberg, 1908.

Ellis-Fermor, Una. The Jacobean Drama: An Interpretation. London, 1936.

England, George, ed. The Towneley Plays, with Introduction and notes by A. W. Pollard. London, 1897.

Fleay, F. G. A Biographical Chronicle of the English Drama 1559-1642. 2 vols. London, 1891.

Furnivall, F. J., ed. The Digby Mysteries. London, 1882.

Gardiner, S. R. The First Two Stuarts and the Puritan Revolution. New York, 1893.

Gerarde, John. The Herball or generall historie of Plantes. London, 1597.

Gittings, Robert. Shakespeare's Rival. London, 1960.

Goldsmid, Edmund, ed. The Last Fight of the Revenge. 2 vols. Edinburgh, 1886.

Greg, W. W. A Bibliography of the English Printed Drama to the Restoration. 4 vols. Oxford, 1939-60.

232

Halliwell, J. O., ed. Ludus Coventriae. London, 1841.

Hazlitt, William, ed. Dodsley's Old English Plays. 15 vols. London, 1874-76.

Higgins, Michael. "The Development of the 'Senecal Man,'" Review of English Studies, XXXIII (1947), 24-33.

Josephus, Flavius. The Famous Workes of Josephus, trans. Thomas Lodge. London, 1602.

Landau, Marcus. "Die Dramen von Herodes und Mariamne," Zeitschrift für vergleichende Literaturgeschichte, N. F., IX (Weimar, 1896), 185ff.

Larkey, Sanford V., M.D., and Thomas Pyles, ed. An Herbal[1525]. New York, 1941.

Lee, Sir Sidney. A Life of William Shakespeare. London, 1908.

Lyon, J. H. H. A Study of The Newe Metamorphosis. New York, 1919.

Markham, Gervase. Devoreux, or Vertues teares. London 1597.

_____. The English Arcadia. 2 pts. London, 1607, 1613.

_____. A Health to the Gentlemanly Profession of Serving-Men. London, 1598; rprt. Oxford, 1931.

_____. Honour in his Perfection. London, 1624.

_____. Marie Magdalens Lamentations. London, 1601.

_____. The most Famous...Historie, of...Meruine. London, 1612.

_____. The Poem of Poems, or Sions Muse. London, 1596.

_____. Rodomonths Infernall. London, 1607.

Markham, Gervase and William Sampson. The True Tragedy of Herod and Antipater, with the Death of Faire Marriam. London, 1622.

Massinger, Philip. The Plays of Philip Massinger, ed. W. Gifford. 4 vols. London, 1805.

Murray, Sir J. A. H., ed. The Oxford English Dictionary. 13 vols. Oxford, 1933.

Parker, R. E. "The Reputation of Herod in Early English Literature," Speculum, VIII (1933), 59-67.

Poynter, F. N. L. A Bibliography of Gervase Markham 1568?-1637. Oxford, 1962.

Purvis, J. S., ed. The York Cycle of Mystery Plays. London, 1957.

Reynolds, George Fullmer. The Staging of Elizabethan Plays at the Red Bull Theater 1605-1625. New York, 1940.

Ribner, Irving. The English History Play in the Age of Shakespeare. Princeton, 1957.

_____ Jacobean Tragedy. London, 1962.

Sallust. The Conspiracy of Catiline and The War of Jugurtha, trans. Thomas Heywood, with an Introduction by Charles Whibley. New York, 1924.

Sampson, William. The Vow Breaker in Materialien zur Kunde des älteren Englischen Dramas, ed. Hans Wallrath. Louvain, 1914; rprt. Vaduz, 1963.

Schelling, Felix E. Elizabethan Drama 1558-1642. 2 vols. New York, 1910.

Seneca. Seneca's Tragedies, trans. Frank Justus Miller. 2 vols. Cambridge, Massachusetts, 1953.

Shakespeare. The Complete Plays and Poems of William Shakespeare, ed. W. A. Neilson and C. J. Hill. Cambridge, Massachusetts, 1942.

Silbermann, A. M. Untersuchungen über die Quellen des Dramas The True Tragedy of Herod and Antipater. Wittenberg, 1922.

Sophocles. Sophocles, trans. Thomas Francklin. New York, 1834.

Stephen, Sir Leslie and Sir Sidney Lee, ed. The Dictionary of National Biography. 22 vols. Oxford, 1917.

Tomlinson, Warren E. Der Herodes-Charakter im englischen Drama. Leipzig, 1934.

Tourneur, Cyril. The Works of Cyril Tourneur, ed. Allardyce Nicoll. London, 1929.

Valency, Maurice J. The Tragedies of Herod and Mariamne. New York, 1940.

Wallace, C. W. "Gervase Markham, dramatist," Shakespeare Jahrbuch, XLVI (1910), 347-350.

Wells, Henry W. Elizabethan and Jacobean Playwrights. New York, 1939.

Wickham, Glynne. Early English Stages 1300 to 1660. 2 vols. New York, 1963.

Wright, Thomas, ed. The Chester Plays. 2 vols. London, 1843-47.